A modern-day marriage miracle: A tribute to the power of God and clinical skills in healing marriages and people.

—**Pat Love,** Ed.D.
Co-author *How to Improve Your Marriage Without Talking About It* and *The Truth About Love*

No matter where you are in your relationship, "*Rebuilding Broken Bridges*" gives you proven strategies and time tested wisdom to create a brighter future. John Wagner is a true master. He understands what it takes to rebuild a marriage because he has done it and now he is making it available for the rest of the world to see.

—**Dr. Dave Martin**
America's #1 Christian Success Coach
& author of *The 12 Traits of the Greats*

This is an inspiring story about faith in God made operational by clinical skills which saved and transformed a marriage. It should bring hope to all its readers.

—**Harville Hendrix,** Ph.D.
Author: *Getting the Love You Want: A Guide for Couples*

# REBUILDING BROKEN BRIDGES
## FOR COUPLES

"This is an inspiring story about faith in God made operational by clinical skills which saved and transformed a marriage. It should bring hope to all its readers."
—**Harville Hendrix, Ph.D.** Author: *Getting the Love You Want: A Guide For Couples*

# REBUILDING BROKEN BRIDGES
## FOR COUPLES
*Giving Hope for Relationships in Crisis*

## JOHN WAGNER, M.S.

© 2011 by John Wagner. All rights reserved.

WinePress Publishing (PO Box 428, Enumclaw, WA 98022) functions only as book publisher. As such, the ultimate design, content, editorial accuracy, and views expressed or implied in this work are those of the author.

No part of this publication may be reproduced, stored in a retrieval system, or transmitted in any way by any means—electronic, mechanical, photocopy, recording, or otherwise—without the prior permission of the copyright holder, except as provided by USA copyright law.

Unless otherwise noted, all Scriptures are taken from the *New King James Version*. Copyright © 1982 by Thomas Nelson, Inc. Used by permission. All rights reserved.

Scripture references marked AMPLIFIED are taken from the *Amplified® Bible*, Copyright © 1954, 1958, 1962, 1964, 1965, 1987 by The Lockman Foundation. Used by permission. (www.Lockman.org)

Scripture references marked NIV are taken from the *Holy Bible, New International Version®, NIV®*. Copyright © 1973, 1978, 1984 by Biblica, Inc.™ Used by permission of Zondervan. All rights reserved worldwide. www.zondervan.com

Scripture references marked NASB are taken from the *New American Standard Bible*, © 1960, 1963, 1968, 1971, 1972, 1973, 1975, 1977, 1995 by The Lockman Foundation. Used by permission.

ISBN 13: 978-1-4141-1773-7
ISBN 10: 1-4141-1773-6
Library of Congress Catalog Card Number: 2010904214

This work is dedicated to Susan, the woman of my dreams, who saw a vision and was willing to help resurrect our marriage to give me a blessed life that is safe and passionate. I also want to dedicate this work to my adult kids, Jeff, Kimberly, and Kristin, who have given us nine beautiful grandchildren. To Harville Hendrix, whose work was an inspiration to heal our marriage, to Pat Love, whose friendship and training has inspired me to go to the next level, to Dwight Bain, whose encouragement to do this work and not quit was a blessing, and to Lee Warren and Dawn Lipthrott, whose ideas inspired me in so many ways.

And most importantly, to my Father in heaven, whose unconditional love forgave me all the wrongs that caused so much pain and lifted me up to help other couples heal.

# CONTENTS

Preface . . . . . . . . . . . . . . . . . . . . . . . . . . . . . . . . . . . . . . . . . . . . ix

Chapter One: Rebuilding a Broken Bridge. . . . . . . . . . . . . . . . 1
Chapter Two: The Mystery of Marriage Covenant . . . . . . . . . . . . . 19
Chapter Three: Ah! Young Love: There's Banana Splits,
   Then Splitting of Assets . . . . . . . . . . . . . . . . . . . . . . . . . . . . 41
Chapter Four: Liposuction of Your Soul—Your Mind,
   Emotions, and Will . . . . . . . . . . . . . . . . . . . . . . . . . . . . . 59
Chapter Five: If You Want To Be Right, You're Going
   To Be Lonely! . . . . . . . . . . . . . . . . . . . . . . . . . . . . . . . . . . . 71
Chapter Six: Slaying the Giant-killers in Your Relationship . . . . . . 85
Chapter Seven: After the Affair. . . . . . . . . . . . . . . . . . . . . . . 101
Chapter Eight: The Rest of Your Life Can Be the Best of Your Life . 111
Chapter Nine: Is Real Love or Vintage Love Possible? . . . . . . . . 129
Chapter Ten: How to Turn the Fizzle Back into a Sizzle! . . . . . . . 143

Bibliography . . . . . . . . . . . . . . . . . . . . . . . . . . . . . . . . . . . 151

Endnotes . . . . . . . . . . . . . . . . . . . . . . . . . . . . . . . . . . . 153

# PREFACE

*REBUILDING BROKEN BRIDGES* aims to give hope to those who are struggling and want to find the relationship of their dreams. It also puts forth biblical ideas on healthy marriages and joins them with the latest research in relationships. A couple's model for therapy, Imago Relationship Therapy, was developed by Harville Hendrix and Helen Hunt and is presented to give a Christian perspective on this topic.

When discussing biblical concepts in this book, I am not writing from a legalistic perspective. Rather, I am writing from the perspective of seeking God's wisdom. When we seek his wisdom, we can understand why God opposes divorce or sex outside of marriage. When we approach this legalistically, we begin judging individuals and using Scripture to shame them into submission. That will not work on any meaningful level.

Some readers may be offended by these concepts, so I ask you to approach this book with an open mind. My wife and I dream of having an impact in our world in the area of marriages and relationships. Our vision is "to save the children of our world by healing relationships." It is critical that the body of Christ begin walking in the love of God and the Spirit of Christ, instead of judging and shaming one another.

When looking at the idea of obedience, we need to look at the Greek words the Bible uses. The English language does not always convey their original meanings. One word, for example, is *peitharcheo,* which refers to obedience to authority. Yet this word is not used for the obedience of faith. The word *hupakoe* is the word used for obedience of faith. This word is a compound of "hupo," a preposition, and "akouo," a verb meaning to hear or understand. Putting the two together, this word translated *obedience* means "to submit to and hearken to what is said."

The very Greek word itself shows us we cannot have obedience apart from hearing in such a way as to hearken and obey what is heard. In the beginning of Genesis, the most obvious thing about God is He speaks! "And God said, Let there be light; and there was light" (Gen. 1:3 AMPLIFIED). In the New Testament, the apostle Paul tells us that "faith comes by hearing, and what is heard comes by the preaching of Christ" (Rom. 10:17 AMPLIFIED). Obedience comes by faith and hearing God. When we hear the word that God speaks today, it gives us the power to accomplish what God has spoken.

When I use the idea of obedience, I refer to hearing God and then, through faith, taking a step by hearing his voice and guidance. God is the ultimate mentor, the ultimate life coach, the ultimate therapist. Many times we miss our destiny by not listening to that still, small voice inside and then stepping out in obedience and faith to reach our full potential.

I sincerely hope that this book motivates readers to be all they can be in their marriage, relationships, family, life, and career.

## Why Is Marriage So Important?

Marriage trends in the United States show that beginning in the late 1960s and early 1970s, marriage rates began to decline. From 1970 to the present, the marriage rate has decreased by fifty percent. The trend also shows that divorce and unwed childbearing significantly increased. Today four out of ten births are to unwed mothers.

## Why Marriage Matters

In 2002, a report from U. S. Family Scholars drew twenty-one conclusions from the Social Services. These are a few of those conclusions:

- Marriage increases the likelihood that fathers have good relationships with their children.
- Growing up outside an intact marriage increases the likelihood that children will themselves divorce or become unwed parents.
- Divorce and unmarried childbearing increases poverty for both children and mothers.
- Parental divorce or failures to marry appears to increase a child's risk of failure in school.
- Marriage is associated with better health and with lower rates of injury, illness, disability, alcohol and substance abuse, delinquent behavior, and depression.

## Does Divorce Make People Happy?

A 2002 study done by Waite, Browning, Doherty, Gallagher, Leu, and Stanley shows that divorce does not make people happier. Here are some of the study results:

Unhappily married adults who divorced or separated were no happier, on average, than unhappily married adults who stayed married. Even unhappy spouses who had divorced and remarried were no happier than unhappy spouses who stayed married. This was true even after controlling for race, age, gender, and income. Divorce is usually not the best choice for solutions to marriage pain.

Divorce did not reduce symptoms of depression for unhappily married adults, raise their self-esteem, or increase their sense of mastery, compared to unhappy spouses who stayed married. This was true even after controlling for race, age, gender, and income.

Staying married did not typically trap unhappy spouses in violent relationships. Eighty-six percent of unhappily married adults reported no violence in their relationship. Ninety-three percent of unhappy spouses who avoided divorce reported no violence in their marriage five years later. The majority of marriages were not violent. (Source: American Institute of Values—www. americanvalues.org)

*Chapter One*

# REBUILDING A BROKEN BRIDGE

AS I SAT in our backyard with my eyes closed, I barely felt the heat of the Florida summer afternoon. Maybe the pain would just fade away if I just kept my eyes closed. Tears needed to come, so why fight it? I opened my eyes and stared into the sky in a daze as the sadness welling up within me brought endless sobbing. My eyes were so filled with tears that things looked blurry as I tried to focus on my surroundings. One painful thought began pulling me out of my shock and numbness: My wife Susan had just walked out on me after eleven years of marriage.

Time stands still in moments like that. One minute feels like an hour, an hour feels like a day, a day feels like a week, and a week feels like a month. Like a merry-go-round spinning out of control, my mind raced through thoughts of my life, showing me flashes of bad choices. My mind was obsessed with all my failures. Through my mental fog a fear began to swirl up from my inner self. *This must be what a nervous breakdown feels like.* My breathing was labored, and my heart palpitated. A dizzying sense left me paralyzed as I sobbed uncontrollably.

As I looked around the yard hoping with all my heart that I would see her coming back, my hands shook and my heart ached. If only she would come out into the yard. But she didn't come out that back door, no matter how much I hoped for. Finally, I looked skyward—toward the only answer that was left. I cried out to God, asking him to forgive me for the sin I had committed.

The first month after I realized my marriage to Susan was ending, I lost all sense of time. Some days I would just walk around crying, remembering nothing but being in a foggy daze. How could this be happening? We were active in our church. I knew God's Word and could quote Scripture with anyone. We even had a ministry helping couples. Yet there we were, on the threshold of being total failures in our sacred covenant of marriage before God.

What led to this devastating point? I had been aware of a few of our problems as they were happening. But much of the understanding I will relate in this book came only years later as I reflected on those pivotal events. We had come into our relationship with a lot of baggage. But like most couples who fall in love, we were not aware of how that baggage would eventually affect us.

Susan and I went from being so in love and passionate about our relationship to feeling emotionally unsafe with each other. When couples reach this point, they feel disconnected and avoid relational intimacy. In our relationship, most of the issues were my own, and I unknowingly sabotaged our marriage. At the time I tended to blame Susan, and I took little if any responsibility for my part in our difficulties. . 

For a man who is performance-oriented, as most men are, failing as a protector or provider erodes the very core of our masculinity. The shame we feel leads to a fatalistic philosophy: "Nothing I do will be good enough."

At the time I thought my wife was criticizing me. Only years later did I realize the problem arose from the issues I brought into the marriage. She was just trying to get me to show up for our relationship in the way she needed me to. I took her expression of her legitimate needs as unwarranted criticism. Men and women are wired differently, as Pat Love writes in her book *How to Improve Your Marriage without Talking about It*. Unfortunately, at that time I lacked any relationship education. Oh, I tried to save our sinking ship. But I had neither the right attitude nor the right tools.

Still, God wasn't done with me. In Romans 12:2 Paul wrote, "Do not be conformed to this world, but be transformed by the renewing of your mind, so that you may prove what the will of God is, that which is good, acceptable, and perfect" (NASB). And the Master was about to transform my mind.

My wife had good reason to leave me. Not only had I been unfaithful to her, but she discovered I had also been having an affair for some time. My behavior was selfish, deceptive, and manipulative. How can an individual betray a person you marry and love? It would be some time before I understood the answer to this question.

When Susan confronted me, at first I denied it. I was so out of touch with how my unfaithfulness had devastated her, I was concerned only that I had been caught. Worse, when she tried to confront me, I would react in anger. At the time I didn't realize my anger came from my shame and humiliation. I had betrayed my wife and the covenant we entered into when we were married. Getting angry when we are confronted by the person we have betrayed is the way many men act when we get caught. What is the logic in that reaction?

I stopped the affair. But like a lot of couples, we swept the situation under the rug. Part of that is the responsibility of the partner committing the offense, because they think they can repair the relationship. There are many reasons a betrayed spouse might fear dealing with the real issue. Often the reason is economic because as a mother, the woman fears isolation or financial hardship. That is such a sad position to feel trapped in. Though we tried going to counseling, Susan and I never really dealt with the pain of my infidelity. Nothing seemed to help us.

Months later, Susan found children's toys in the back of my car. She was convinced I was still seeing the woman. I tried to explain that I was innocent. As a real estate broker, I had been showing houses to a couple, and their children had left some toys in the back seat. Susan didn't believe me. Who could blame her, as I didn't know how to earn her trust. I believed that trust should just happen. I felt my infidelity lay in the past—and now we just needed to move forward. Today in my counseling practice, I often hear statements like that from men who have been unfaithful. I also find that few couples ever develop a strategy for redeveloping trust in the relationship.

A few weeks later, Susan left. I was in such denial and shock. To me, our relationship seemed fine. How could I have been so wrong?

In reality, we were not fine. We were broken, and I had no idea how disconnected we were. Now I remember this when couples come to my office for help with their marriages. One person thinks everything is fine, and the other is miserable. The fact is, I heard Susan, but I never really *heard* her.

As I walked around in a daze of total depression after she left me, I couldn't understand how this could be happening. I was so selfish and in such denial. I never once thought of the horrible pain she must have felt when she discovered my unfaithfulness. All I remember is making a statement I would later understand as the alcoholic creed: "I was sick and tired of being sick and tired."

One day as the sun was going down, with darkness closing in and suffering unbearable pain, I fell on my face before God and began a new and foreign journey. I would encounter something powerful that would change my entire life: *repentance*.

## Step One: Repentance

If only we Christians could grasp the cleansing power of repentance—of being sorry for our shortcomings and wanting to start anew.[1] This is not repentance as a single event, but as a journey we can walk throughout our lives. Repentance is not beating ourselves over the head because of our behavior—all that does is deepen our shame. Repentance is not some ritual we go through to let us off the hook from facing the consequences of our behavior. Repentance is not asking God to forgive us on Sunday for what we plan to do on Monday. God may forgive us, but we will still have to experience the consequences of our actions and unhealthy choices. Repentance is a process of change from my way to God's way. I believe it is a total surrender to seek his will for our lives. When we spend time with God, when we know God and not just know about him, when we meditate on the Word, step out in faith and let hope and patience work, we can evolve to the place we need to be.

The repentant voyage is a day-by-day, week-by-week, and month-by-month journey. The Bible says a "godly sorrow produces repentance leading to salvation" (NKJV). Repentance leads to a person being cleansed, and I was certainly going through a cleansing that would change my heart for the rest of my life. At the time, however, I had no idea of the eventual outcome. This account of our journey may seem simple at first, but this was the most difficult experience I have ever been through. My goal is to stay on that journey the rest of my days.

When we begin to seek the very presence of God and ask for forgiveness and wisdom to guide our steps, an empowerment comes upon us that cannot be described. Such empowerment can only come from the power of God's Holy Spirit inside us.

I had been full of pride. Although I can't blame the profession I was in, it didn't help. I had been in the entertainment business since I was fourteen, and I traveled the world performing concerts and making television appearances as a singer with a vocal group called The Diamonds. We had sixteen Top 40 hits during the Doo-Wop era of the late 1950s and early 1960s. While I played thirteen instruments, my main one was the tenor saxophone. All of this success fed my ego.

The Diamonds –(Glen Stetson, John Wagner, John Davis, Mike Douglas-1990)

Music was much of my life. It was a gift I inherited, and when I stepped on stage, my alter ego took over and masked all the inadequacies I felt. People would look at me and think I had it made. We would come off stage to adoring fans. Few knew that inside my adult self, I was like a crying little boy. I was looking for love in all the wrong places, as the Johnny Lee song states. For decades I hid behind the tenor saxophone.

I had not been the man, the father, or the husband God wanted me to be. And I didn't have a clue how to be that man. I was a phony Christian in so many ways. I talked the talk, but in many areas of my life didn't walk the walk. I used to hear a message from the fifth chapter of Ephesians that a husband was to love his wife as Christ loved the church. Would someone tell me how to do that?

As I began spending daily time on my face before God, seeking his voice, forgiveness, and perfect will for my life, my heart began to change. I could sense the Holy Spirit cleansing me from the inside. Entering into a covenant with God, I told him that whether or not Susan ever came back, I wanted to be his man. At the time, I had no idea what a pivotal point that was in our journey as a couple. I was letting her go. She didn't deserve to be with a man displaying my kind of behavior.

I made another key decision. I went to my pastor and the elders of our church and confessed my sins according to James 5:16: "Confess your sins to each other and pray for each other so that you may be healed. The prayer of a righteous man is powerful and effective" (NIV). I wanted healing, but being on my knees confessing this horrible sin before these men I respected was one of the most difficult things I can remember. Yet I needed to perform this act of remorse. I had failed more than just my wife—I had failed them by my actions. As I released the weight of the secret I had kept, I broke down in front of them. As they saw my remorse, they put their arms around me and encouraged me to continue on my new journey. It was cleansing to get my secret out in the open. I was discovering that carrying the weight of this secret had burdened me far more than I realized. As painful as it was to go through, I was being set free by the truth.

There apparently had been a dark side of my life that I battled for years and didn't know how to face. I believe in earlier years I had been fighting a compulsion, almost like an addiction to love. I was so naïve in those earlier years that I could not see that issue. One would have thought a person could be aware when they have a number of failed relationships. I might have been aware in some way but didn't know how to rise above that. This is more of the type of baggage we bring into a marriage relationship.

Through counseling I began working on my deepest issues, and I became totally transparent in dealing with them. Transparency is not easy, yet it is so freeing to let go of the shame that binds you and to experience what John 8:32 says: "You will know the Truth, and the Truth will set you free" (AMPLIFIED).

I had asked my counselors to be truthful and not pull any punches. They didn't! At times that was difficult. When we face the darkness in our lives, it is like sandpaper being rubbed across our skin. That is a painful process, but the journey to healing requires going through pain. In counseling, the defensive layers I had developed through life scripts were peeled away to get to my core issues. The infidelity was my selfish way to get validation for who I was. Life scripts are masks we develop to hide the self-hatred we feel from the shame that binds us.

Many of our friends began seeing a changed heart in me. Many, including one of Susan's best friends, were praying for us and the restoration of our marriage. At the time, even though they knew what I had done, no one had any idea of the devastating hurt and anger Susan had gone through.

But God had not yet touched Susan. She was not impressed by any changes in me—so not impressed that she divorced me. I recall sitting in her attorney's office making the statement that one day we would be back together. This really angered her, especially when her attorney said the same thing. Yet God was not done with either of us.

## Step Two: Release

I then entered into the second step of my journey. That step was release. One evening as I walked around my neighborhood, I realized I needed to release the situation to God—to give him my life and my marriage. Sometimes we try to manipulate God with our prayers, as if he doesn't know everything we are thinking. But sometimes, when we have petitioned God with our prayers, we have to release those requests for God to work them out.

I believe that when I did that the spiritual forces of the universe were released so God could begin working on the healing of our relationship. At the time of this release I could not say I prophetically saw this happening. I just knew I had to cast all my cares upon him who cares for me (1 Pet. 5:7). One reason I had to learn to let go was that my personality was very manipulative, and that would have to change.

## Susan's Story

It just couldn't be true. "I'm telling you Susan," said my good friend Jan, "he's seeing somebody else. I saw them together last night, and it sickened me."

The pain drove me to my knees. My mouth opened in an attempt to scream, but my stomach was twisted in too many knots for any sound to escape. *John is having an affair? How dare he!* I fell on my knees. This couldn't be happening. He would never betray me like that. How could he do that to me, us, our family?

My thoughts swung from rage to depression to near-hysteria. I remember throwing myself on our bed and crying for what seemed like hours. I picked up the phone to call John—and started screaming at him. When your heart has been pierced by betrayal, most of us lose control of our emotions. Grace and forgiveness were the furthest ideas from my mind. I wanted to pay him back; my rage was one way of doing that. In moments when we lose all control of our rationale, we often do things like that, somehow thinking we are paying someone back. The truth is, we are not.

You think because you are a Christian and get married that everything will be wonderful. When you are so in love, you think this connection will last forever. What we don't realize when we get married is that we are selfish. For a marriage to succeed, we need some basic tools. We need information and understanding on why we are attracted to each other, how to communicate with each other, and what we need from each other. We need to learn how to be married and how to raise children.

When we married, John and I both had unresolved business from our past. But we didn't realize it. I look back and wish we had received help and healing before I left him. Actually, I didn't leave at first. Somehow I thought we could crawl out of this hole. So I gave John the benefit of the doubt, thinking we could heal. Months later, still not trusting him, I found toys in his car and was convinced he had never stopped the affair. I left him then, only to find out later that he had stopped seeing the woman months before.

John and I first met at Calvary Assembly's singles ministry in Winter Park, Florida. We had both been previously married. I had two daughters (ages eight and ten), and John had a son (age twelve). He asked me out for coffee. When I got home that night, I said to myself, "No, he is not the one." We just didn't click. I didn't realize he felt the same way.

A year went by. With my parents, my children, and a prayer partner, we went on vacation to Heritage USA in South Carolina While there, my prayer partner had a vision. Visions were new to me. She told me she knew who my husband was to be. She told me he was John Wagner. She saw us older—in a chapel building. John was sitting on the platform looking very distinguished, and I was speaking. The people in the audience had slanted eyes. She asked the Lord if the people were Asian, and God said no; Susan is opening the eyes of the deceived. I was taken back with this vision as John and I were not even talking—let alone dating.

I didn't believe my friend at first. I got back home with my family on a Sunday evening. The next morning, John called me. I was shocked because I had not seen him for a year. We began dating, and this time it clicked. Eventually he asked me to marry him, and I said yes. How could I have not fallen in love with him? He was so charming, charismatic, spontaneous, and passionate about life. Having a family was so important to him. John adopted my daughters and raised them as if they were his biological children.

Years later, when I learned John was having an affair, I thought my world was coming to an end. I can remember saying to God, "You gave this vision to me; how could this be happening?" A mistake must have been made. The pain was unbearable. I didn't want to live this way. No words can describe the pain you experience when your dream comes apart. I can't begin to describe those horrible hours. Months later, I was still so angry and hurt that when I saw those toys in John's car, I would not talk to him and I left. Convinced the affair was still going on, I would not believe him.

During the next year, I stayed angry and hurt and filed for divorce. Some friends were telling me that John had been working on himself and having a heart change, but I could not trust that with what had happened. Time went on and John's son, Jeff, was getting married. Jeff wanted me to be there when he got married, so I accepted his invitation with some apprehension. Little did I know what was to happen.

As we both showed up at the wedding, a miracle happened. In church earlier that day, the Holy Spirit came upon me. I couldn't stop weeping. I wept through the service and all through lunch. I did not understand why I was crying, but I felt the Holy Spirit upon me. I believe God was softening my heart so that when John and I saw each other, I would be able to talk to him.

After the wedding we stayed in the sanctuary and talked endlessly. A week later, we met for dinner. That evening when I got home, the Holy Spirit said to me, "Are you going to live your life your way, or are you going to live it my way?" Those words penetrated my being and I knew God was bringing that vision back into my heart. He was saying to me, "I have a plan for your life."

## John's Story

Months went by and nothing happened. I went on with my life until one day God touched Susan's heart and mine. A most amazing thing about this miracle was that it occurred at my son's wedding—reminding me that the first miracle Jesus performed was also at a wedding. That day as we met, we were both apprehensive. We had not communicated for nearly a year, but at the wedding we started talking. We talked so much we even missed part of the reception. We began discussing the possibility of exploring how to put our relationship back together.

## Step Three: Obedience

Talking with Susan again brought both of us to a third step, which is obedience. God was putting us back together—whether we felt like it or not. We knew deep down that our destiny was to be together. But we were not two people running in slow motion across a meadow embracing in the middle and having skyrockets go off. This was a scary time. I had not yet earned Susan's trust, and a lot of healing still had to occur. From one day to the next, we did not know what was happening between us. But the decision we made to become obedient began our healing process.

When some Christians think of obedience it is usually in the context of being obedient to Old Testament laws and commandments. That kind of obedience might also be thought of as legalism. But the New Testament book of Hebrews tells us that no one could keep the law in every detail. Because of that, Jesus came to fulfill the law. Christ gave his followers only one commandment, and that was to love him and our brothers.

Applying that to our decision, Susan and I were being obedient to love each other. Refusing to take that step would not condemn us or put us beyond the pale. But by taking that step, we were putting ourselves in a position to be blessed. We were not aware of this as we took these steps, however. Wouldn't it be a wonderful world if we all walked in that love instead of judging one another and gossiping? Think of the incredible blessings we would receive.

We made a commitment to love each other, and our feelings gradually began to come back. One problem in our microwave Western culture is that we are oriented to events and feelings. As long as there are the feelings of love, we think we are with the right person. When those feelings are no longer there, we are not with the right person. The modern mass media has programmed us to believe that love is confirmed on the basis of our feelings.

The statistics show how much we believe this. We know that about half of all first-time marriages end in divorce, but what we don't hear is that sixty-five percent of second-time marriages and about seventy percent of third-time marriages also end in divorce. If divorce were the answer, then these statistics for second and third marriages would be going the other way.

When we make a decision to love our spouse, the byproduct of that decision is our emotions or feelings. But our own "selfness" can make us incapable of making that decision. There are times when we are so self-oriented that the pain we feel in a ruptured relationship keeps us from the very hope that can bring a rebirth to that relationship.

I believe there are times when a marriage between two hurting people has to die before a resurrection can happen. In the middle of an argument with your beloved, you are not feeling great love. But when we make a decision on the other side of that argument to love that person, the feelings come back. Put that idea in a larger piece of time and make the same decision—and the feelings will return. In therapy this is one of the most difficult concepts for individuals to understand.

Part of our journey to be obedient was putting to work a process we learned from a model of marriage counseling developed in the 1980s by Dr. Harville Hendrix and his wife, Helen Hunt. They called it "Imago Relationship Therapy." Hendrix's first book *Getting the Love You Want* explains this process with one of the main skills being the "Couple's Dialogue," where a couple engages in a structured conversation. The communication skills we learned began to help us understand the core issues in our power struggle which led to the tearing apart of our marriage. (When I mention communication skills, I mean learning to connect with each other at a deeper, more intimate level. We had talked for years. Couples talk all of the time, but they rarely connect and truly understand each other.)

Eventually an exciting day came to pass. After a painful year and a half, Susan and I decided to get remarried. Had a vote been taken in our church, we would have probably been voted the couple least likely to succeed. Our remarriage was not just an exchange of vows, but a whole church celebration, with Susan walking down the aisle wearing the wedding dress our daughter wore at her wedding the year before.

Susan was gorgeous as she walked down the aisle. My son Jeff, was my best man. Susan's friend Jackie, who had prayed for us through our ordeal, was her bridesmaid. The ceremony was truly a celebration to a victory of God and the process of Imago Relationship Therapy in our lives, offering hope to others who may walk through a similar crisis. As she walked down the aisle, Susan was thinking what a tribute to God's victory this was. She was thinking what a beautiful story of how two people who walked through such bitterness, lack of forgiveness, anger, and pain could come to the victorious place of being healed, set free, and totally in love with each other.

**JOHN AND SUSAN**-our remarriage picture

## Healing Relationships

In our journey we learned how to make history actually become history in our lives and relationship. What we discovered was that in order to heal the dysfunction in our family, we first had to heal the dysfunction in our relationship. Ideally, this healing starts from the head of the family and works down, not from the feet up. This lesson, one I have walked through myself, now serves as the basis for the work I do with couples. If a husband and wife are not in harmony, it is difficult to have harmony in the rest of the family. 1 Peter 3:8–9 states, "Finally, all of you, live in harmony with one another; be sympathetic, love as brothers, be compassionate and humble. Do not repay evil with evil or insult with insult, but with blessing, because to this you were called so that you may inherit a blessing"(NIV). In other words, we are to inherit a blessing by learning to bless others and not control them. How difficult that is in the middle of pain and hurt!

The healing Susan and I went through was only part of our journey. With my selfish behavior, I had hurt many people. Most importantly, I hurt my kids, who were young adults by this time. And I also hurt Susan's parents. I knew I had a long way to go to earn their trust. One of our daughters wouldn't talk to me for two years after we were married and Susan's father didn't want me on his property. I could not blame them for feeling that way.

As our remarriage date was December 7, when Susan's dad told her he didn't want me at their home, she was not going to go see them at Christmas. I told her she had to maintain that relationship with her parents as we never know when they won't be with us any longer. The next year her father went through major health problems with his heart. I would go to the hospital and stay in the lobby praying for him. I walked in unconditional love, and I believe God honored that. Shortly before he died we made a connection and her father forgave me.

I had to do the same with my daughter, and eventually we made a reconnection. Behavior has consequences, however, and to this day I am so totally aware that I need to honor her and walk in unconditional love.

The beauty of a repentant journey is that God gives the grace and wisdom not to expect that we're entitled to forgiveness. With the new heart God had given me, I knew I had to walk in unconditional love with everyone I had hurt. That kind of love can only come from the grace (unmerited favor) that God gives us. In time, I earned the trust of those I had hurt in so many ways.

As we began to be healed in our relationship, God gave us both a vision of "saving the children of this world by healing relationships." As our healing grew, our spiritual walk with God grew. We became teammates, not just helpmates. We became best friends and not best enemies. We became prayer warriors earnestly seeking God's will for our future. Our healing was so dramatic that I began to see a vision of helping other couples find the dream relationship we found.

## Following the Vision

When you believe God gives you a vision, step out boldly to claim it. I decided to follow that vision and start graduate school at an age when I should have been thinking of retiring. At age fifty I finished graduate school in psychology. I then began the process of getting licensed, with the goal of being a family therapist and getting my certification in Imago Relationship Therapy. I wanted to help troubled couples by blending biblical teaching with practical application and skills that individuals could understand.

I went to Boise, Idaho, to intern with Ron Dent, a psychologist who trained me in Imago Therapy. My formal Imago training was with Pat Love in Austin, Texas. Pat is the author of *The Emotional Incest Syndrome, Hot Monogamy, The Truth about Love,* and most recently *How to Improve Your Marriage without Talking about It.* That last title is probably every man's dream—the two words men fear the most are "let's talk"!

The vision of saving the children of this world by healing relationships started becoming a reality as we began helping other couples through their struggles. After all, we did not just talk the talk; we had also walked the talk. By God's grace, the power of our testimony has given hope to hundreds of other couples in crisis who saw no way out.

I believe that *couples do not want divorce; they want an end to pain.* If they can find a way to deal with pain, many marriages heading toward divorce can be saved. God has shown me that before we can have a unified family, one based on intimacy, we have to have marriages in harmony. Many couples' power struggles occur because they sabotage their relationships with the baggage brought into that relationship. That baggage creates an emotionally unsafe environment for the pair.

One goal for couples on their journey of healing is to see their partner's world as it is to their partner, rather than to see it only from their own perspective. In other words, to learn what that world is like for one's spouse, not just what you think it is.

When a couple doesn't feel safe with each other, either emotionally or physically, distance begins to develop. And when distance develops, relational intimacy suffers. That is when a couple feels like they are two ships passing in the night without a rudder, feeling like roommates instead of lovers hopeless that they can ever feel love for each other again. The only way to rekindle that intimacy and passion in a marriage is to find a way to redevelop safety so the emotional distance begins to close. The book of James states, "Let every man be quick to hear [a ready listener], slow to speak, slow to take offense and to get angry" (1:19 AMPLIFIED). That is the key to unlock your spouse's heart.

I have yet to see a couple intentionally using these skills who do not find the "relationship of their dreams." Imago Relationship Therapy is the door through which couples can discover harmony, intimacy, and passion. Their children can be saved from drugs, alcohol, suicide, and gangs. I believe in the potential of us all coming together—and walking toward the path of healed children.

Susan and I have not arrived. We do not walk on water. We are on a journey to eventually spend eternity with our Father. Our journey is exciting, romantic, and filled with daily blessings. When marriage is in harmony, couples enjoy many byproducts. Their prayers are no longer hindered, according to First Peter 3:7; financial blessings can be poured out so we can concentrate our energy on the majors rather than the minors. And most importantly, we can join together as husband and wife and become prayer warriors to present our petitions to God

Our goal is to become and stay "warriors for Christ." Repentance, release, and obedience can bring God's blessings and favor as we have never known. Susan and I have come to believe that our transparency in sharing our testimony can bring hope to couples in crisis. In that way we can truly save the children by healing relationships.

The next chapter will reveal the idea and connection of blood covenant in the Bible and how that relates to marriage covenant. *Covenant* is a concept few Americans understand, thus making it difficult to grasp why it is so important in the Bible. For example, if we do not understand what a blood covenant is, how can we understand what having a relationship with God is all about? And beyond that, how can we understand the marriage covenant that is created when we exchange our wedding vows? Explore this vital mystery with us.

*Chapter Two*
___

# THE MYSTERY OF MARRIAGE COVENANT

THE DAY OF celebration had arrived. One part of me was nervous, and the other part was excited. While my fingers were fidgeting and I was sweating profusely, I was also excited about our future together. A paradox! Waiting for the bride must be some type of payback for the groom. Thoughts of "what if she doesn't show up" and "what if she does" raced through my mind. I was staring out a window looking for her—and suddenly she appeared. She looked beautiful, like a movie star, with the wind blowing through her hair, which she had just taken so much time to style. My heart was pounding so hard that I felt like my chest would burst. And then she entered the room. I was blessed. Without a doubt, I was "marrying up."

Then we were sharing our vows and entering into a covenant. I doubt that anyone can describe a couple's emotional intensity in that moment. So many joyous thoughts and fears race through an individual's mind. We think the joy and happiness will last forever. So how did this covenant fail? Where did it go wrong? How did I fall so far? If I had truly understood what God's Word teaches about the concept of the marriage covenant, I could have spared my wife and myself a lot of problems.

Over the years, through my own experience, the training I received, and the experiences of counseling other couples, I was driven to the Word of God for answers about how to prevent such failures in the marriage covenant. The training and experiences helped me look deeper into a lost teaching in the body of Christ today. I offer this book to readers to discover the tools and skills needed to prevent marriages from dying.

Why do some couples succeed and others fail? Is there a secret to a successful marriage? Paul's letter to the Ephesians has some answers in the fifth chapter, verses twenty to thirty-three:

> Giving thanks always for all things to God the Father in the name of our Lord Jesus Christ, submitting to one another in the fear of God. Wives, submit to your own husbands, as to the Lord. For the husband is head of the wife, as also Christ is head of the church; and He is the Savior of the body. Therefore, just as the church is subject to Christ, so let the wives be to their own husbands in everything. Husbands, love your wives, just as Christ also loved the church and gave Himself for her, that He might sanctify and cleanse her with the washing of water by the word, that He might present her to Himself a glorious church, not having spot or wrinkle or any such thing, but that she should be holy and without blemish. So husbands ought to love their own wives as their own bodies; he who loves his wife loves himself. For no one ever hated his own flesh, but nourishes and cherishes it, just as the Lord does the church. For we are members of His body, of His flesh and of His bones. "For this reason a man shall leave his father and mother and be joined to his wife, and the two shall become one flesh." This is a great mystery, but I speak concerning Christ and the church. Nevertheless let each one of you in particular so love his own wife as himself, and let the wife see that she respects her husband (NKJV).

A man leaving his parents and being joined to his wife as one flesh is the mystery of the marriage covenant.

## Becoming One Flesh

This Scripture indicates that a husband and wife become one flesh. This does not mean we become joined body to body. Rather, this joining refers to an emotional and spiritual unity. 1 Thessalonians 5:23 states, "Now may the God of peace Himself sanctify you completely; and may your whole spirit, soul, and body be preserved blameless at the coming of our Lord Jesus Christ" (NKJV). This means that as humans we are "spirit, soul, and body." Our soul is our mind, emotions, and will. The emotional and spiritual unity is the joining of our souls. The term "soul mate" comes from this scriptural concept, and it means a person who is exactly suited to another person.

As we have journeyed through the historical evolvement of romantic love playing a part in our selection of a mate in marriage, the idea of a soul mate has become diffused to mean simply a person we have fallen in love with. But it is much more than that. A soul mate is my best friend, my romantic lover, and my spiritual partner. He or she is the individual God intended me to be with in marriage.

The Ephesians Scripture reiterates the text of Genesis 2:24: "Therefore a man shall leave his father and mother and be joined to his wife, and they shall become one flesh" (NKJV). The concept of being joined to a marriage partner as one flesh speaks of much more than a geographical change of address. I don't believe we can have the marriage and relationship God intends unless we separate ourselves from our family of origin. We cannot truly become united to our spouse without that separation. Until that happens, it is like having two managers with different agendas. We cannot please them both—no matter how talented we are.

I often have couples in my office where the separation I am talking about has not happened. Either one or both of them have never left their father and mother. When this happens it is usually because of an enmeshed family system that continues after an individual gets married. The spouse cannot separate himself or herself from trying to constantly communicate with a parent, even if it intrudes into the marriage. Of course this does not mean avoiding relationships with our family of origin, but those relationships need to be healthy ones with loving boundaries.

Bob and Sally (the names have been changed) represent an extreme example of this enmeshment. They made an appointment with me—and Sally's mother came with them. This was the first time I had ever seen a mother join her daughter for marriage counseling! Sally needed (or thought she needed) to call her mother three to six times every day, and if she didn't, her mother would call her. On the surface that seems innocent enough, except that the motives were not pure. Sally had never separated from her parents, especially her mother. When Sally was flying somewhere, she could not get off the plane without immediately calling her mother to let her know she had arrived. The mother insisted on that. Sally was being obedient to her mother, even though she was a grown woman, married, and successful in her own right.

I am not saying there is something wrong with communicating with one's parents; that is something I did with my own parents until they went to their eternal life with God. Rather, what is wrong and what can cause a serious problem is the continuous obsession to have to connect with one's parents—at the risk of creating a rupture with one's spouse. That obsession can become something close to being an addiction.

Often the motivation to keep in such close contact with parents is fear or anxiety, which might need to be worked through with a professional. None of Sally's family could understand her husband's frustration and anger. His anger and her obsession became a vicious cycle concerning who was right and who was wrong. In my office I told Bob, Sally, and Sally's mother that they were all wrong. Unfortunately, the competition continued over this young women's heart, and the couple eventually divorced. This is just one very sad situation out of thousands and thousands showing what can happen when a mother or father tries to dominate a married, adult child.

Scripture teaches that "They are no longer two but one flesh. Therefore what God has joined together, let not man separate" (Matt. 19:6 NKJV). In essence, a meddling parent is separating a husband and wife. I sometimes wonder how many marriages are affected because people violate this biblical principle.

## Understanding Mystery

The word *mystery* had a different meaning in Paul's time. Today we associate the word with a suspense-filled novel. In Paul's time, the term had a religious association. His use of *mystery* concerning marriage relationships denoted two ideas. First, it was a hidden form of knowledge that can make a marriage what it should be. This use refers to a hidden mystical sense relating to the union between Christ and his church, typified by human marriage. In understanding this relationship between

Christ and his church—understanding the significance of biblical covenant—we find the model for marriage.

Paul's second use of the word *mystery* is that of people acquiring this hidden knowledge by undergoing certain tests and meeting certain conditions. These tests and conditions relate to the concepts involved in covenant and the general association found two-thousand years ago in Christianity as well as in Judaism.

## God's Plan for Marriage

In the book of Deuteronomy, Moses reviews the lifestyle God planned for the children of Israel. Marriage was to be like "heaven on earth." But the prophet Malachi has this warning about how Judah has desecrated not only their marriage relationships but also their relationship with the Lord:

> And this you do with double guilt; you cover the altar of the Lord with tears [shed by your unoffending wives, divorced by you that you might take heathen wives], and with [your own] weeping and crying out because the Lord does not regard your offering any more or accept it with favor at your hand. Yet you ask, Why does He reject it? Because the Lord was witness [to the covenant made at your marriage] between you and the wife of your youth, against whom you have dealt treacherously and to whom you were faithless. Yet she is your companion and the wife of your covenant [made by your marriage vows]. And did not God make [you and your wife] one [flesh]? Did not One make you and preserve your spirit alive? And why [did God make you two] one? Because He sought a godly offspring [from your union]. Therefore take heed to yourselves, and let no one deal treacherously and be faithless to the wife of his youth. For the Lord, the God of Israel says: I hate divorce and marital separation and him who covers his garment [his wife] with violence. Therefore keep a watch upon your spirit [that it may be controlled by My Spirit], that you deal not treacherously and faithlessly [with your marriage mate.
> —Mal. 2:13-16 AMPLIFIED

The people of Judah had failed in their homes and their marriages. This was not due to a lack of religion. In spite of all their prayers, their marriages were failures. We may be preoccupied with religious activities or doing things for Jesus, but this does not always create a successful marriage. In fact, when we preoccupy ourselves with religious activities outside the home, we can actually contribute to the failure of our relationships and marriages. Many individuals mistake their spiritual needs with activity for God, and they lack the wisdom to see the difference between a relationship with God and performing activities for God. Knowing God and knowing about God are two different things. One cannot know God without spending time with him.

## Understand Covenant

The essence of Israel's failure in the close of Malachi 2:14 lies in the word *covenant*: "She is your companion and the wife of your covenant." They viewed marriage as a relationship for which they might set their own standards. Understanding the concept of "covenant" is the secret to assuring success in marriage. Once we forget or ignore this secret, our marriages lose their sanctity, strength, and stability. Our own society today shows the same symptoms.

Author Diana S. Richmond Garland coauthored the book *Covenant Marriage*, which was written in the 1980s. She is presently the dean of social work at Baylor University. We had a telephone conversation on some of the principles in her book and how they relate to the work I was doing in this book. Here are some of the covenant marriage principles we discussed:[1]

### *Covenant Marriage Principles*

- Marriage is a gift from our heavenly Father for us to celebrate here on earth.

- True love of covenant partners is based not on feelings but on loving decisions and behaviors.

- Marriage is a model of how God loves us and enters into a covenant with us. It reflects God's unconditional love, forgiveness, and grace.

# THE MYSTERY OF MARRIAGE COVENANT 25

- Covenant marriage creates an opportunity to exercise our God-given gifts and godly responsibilities in marriage and in all walks of life outside marriage.
- A covenant marriage is an unconditional commitment to our partner and not some type of contract which is based on a mutual obligation.
- Covenant partners share responsibility for meeting each other's need for love and respect.
- Partners grow spiritually as they live out their covenant promises with each other.
- Marriage is a balance of our differences and our similarities.
- Every covenant marriage has a unique identity and a unique meaning and purpose in the mind of God.
- Conflict is a natural part of a marital relationship and can be a source of relationship growth and increased intimacy. In other words, *conflict is growth trying to happen.* This is a concept most individuals in our culture have a difficult time grasping, yet it is one that changes a person's life.
- Covenant partners need to be in a larger community of faith with the opportunity to minister to others in need.

Look back over the principles of covenant marriage.
List the three you would most like to characterize in your marriage.

_____

_____

_____

_____

## A Fuller Revelation of Marriage

And Pharisees came to Him and put Him to the test by asking, Is it lawful and right to dismiss and repudiate and divorce one's wife for any and every cause? He replied, Have you never read that He Who

made them from the beginning made them male and female, and said, For this reason a man shall leave his father and mother and shall be united firmly (joined inseparably) to his wife, and the two shall become one flesh? So they are no longer two, but one flesh. What therefore God has joined together, let not man put asunder (separate). They said to Him, Why then did Moses command [us] to give a certificate of divorce and thus to dismiss and repudiate a wife? He said to them, Because of the hardness (stubbornness and perversity) of your hearts Moses permitted you to dismiss and repudiate and divorce your wives; but from the beginning it has not been so [ordained].
—Matt. 19:3–8 Amplified

## Four Statements Sum Up the Teaching of Jesus Regarding Marriage

1. The form of marriage that had become accepted in Israel under Judaism was below the level of God's will. The people viewed a covenant as horizontal (person-to-person) rather than vertical (between us and our heavenly Father).
2. God's purpose for marriage was expressed when he created man and woman. They were to become one flesh—a metaphor for an emotional and spiritual union.
3. In the initial union of man and woman, they were so perfectly joined that they became "one flesh." This is reached through unconditional love. After the fall of Adam and Eve, however, humanity no longer had the natural ability to love unconditionally; we had to learn how to do that.
4. It is the purpose of Jesus to restore marriage in the lives of his disciples to the original standard revealed at creation. Why hasn't this happened in the body of Christ today? We are his disciples when we yield to him. God was personally involved in the creation and union of Adam and Eve. Too often today we do not yield to the Father and allow him to be involved in our marriages. This involves being connected to God.

An important concept hidden in these verses from Malachi and Matthew is that we have to leave our family source, our family of origin, in order to become one flesh in marriage. The only way we can find secure attachment in marriage is to deal with our family of origin issues. Then we can be joined inseparably to our spouse. God's decision was for Adam to have a mate. Therefore he formed Eve from Adam and presented her to him. And God established the terms of covenant relationship when he united the original pair.

When divorce happens in our society, the result is broken homes. When homes are broken, our children are deeply affected, whether or not we want to believe this. Research by leading child psychologists provides concrete evidence that our children are affected. In turn, our families, culture, and society become deeply wounded. In the late 1980s, Judith Wallerstein (author of *Second Chances: Men, Women, and Children after Divorce*) did a significant study. She could not find any instances of divorce that did not create in children emotional injuries that affected their adult adjustment to life and their intimate relationships. Usually when someone wants out of a marriage, this fact will not be accepted. Instead, people will rationalize themselves out of the marriage. I like what Dr. Phil says about this: We have to "earn our way out of a marriage."

## The Real Problem

Some Christians believe that everything changed when prayer was taken out of schools. Please! God is bigger than that. That ruling reflected a deeper issue in our culture: humanism. At the end of World War II, the divorce rate increased dramatically—and has been at the present rate for more than fifty years. Fifty years of broken homes is why our society is in its current mess. Suicide, drug addiction, and alcoholism are the result of broken homes and the pain that children have grown up with. This deception reaches all families, even those that have never experienced divorce.

I have never been against prayer anywhere or at anytime. But sometimes Christians fix their eyes on the wrong goal. What we need is more committed Christians running for elective office and bringing to bear their Christian perspective on society.

## The Goal of Covenant Marriage is to Build a Society Where Love, Joy, and Peace Exist Generation to Generation

The first covenant with Jesus is found in Isaiah 1:18: "'Come now, and let us reason together,' says the Lord. 'Though your sins are like scarlet, they shall be as white as snow; though they are red like crimson, they shall be like wool'" (AMPLIFIED).

From the creation to 1400 BC, humanity was justified by faith. In 1400 BC, the Law was given to Moses, and it remained in effect until approximately AD 27, when Jesus was crucified. "For the law was given through Moses, but grace and truth came through Jesus Christ" (John 1:17 NKJV). The Old Testament transformed into the New Testament, and the old covenant gave way to the new covenant. The Law was not a new revelation but a spiritual revelation written on stone. The New Testament revelation is about a relationship written not on stone but in *our hearts*. God has written the new law in our minds and in our hearts. It is the relationship between Christ and the body of Christ, and between the individual and collective relationships within the body of Christ. If our marriages break down, this significantly affects our relationships within the body of Christ, and thus our relationship with Christ.

Marriage is a covenant between God, a man, and a woman. To see this look at the following Scriptures:

> "This is the covenant I will make with the house of Israel after that time," declares the Lord. "I will put my law in their minds and write it on their hearts. I will be their God, and they will be my people."
> —Jer. 31:31-34 NIV

> "Though the mountains be shaken and hills be removed, yet my unfailing love for you will not be shaken nor my covenant of peace be removed," says the Lord, who has compassion on you.
> —Isa. 54:5-10 NIV

> Therefore know that the Lord your God, He is God, the faithful God who keeps covenant and mercy for a thousand generations with those who love Him and keep His commandments.
> —Deut. 7:6-9 NKJV

God prefers a covenant people. A godly marriage is a covenant between God, a man, and a woman. A godly marriage is a partnership, not a merger. The Trinity (Father, Son, and Holy Spirit) is a wonderful example of a partnership working to the maximum potential. The Father is the life source of the Trinity, making decisions and commands, while the Son is the Word speaking forth those commands. The Holy Spirit is the working force or agent on the earth who brings the Word into fruition. This is a great example for the husband and wife. As there is one entity called the Trinity, there are three separate parts of the Trinity that become one. In the marriage covenant there is also one entity, but a separate husband and wife who become one—the ultimate team.

If we change any of the godly ideas of covenant marriage we lose stability, the real meaning, and the sanctity of the institution of marriage. When we change the attitude of covenant in marriage, we lose. Not necessarily in the short duration, but over the long run.

We change the attitude of covenant in marriage when a partner's faithfulness to their partner is based on our feelings. A marriage based on feelings is very insecure. But marriage covenant produces consistency, stability, and maturity. You cannot run from your problems in covenant—for God will make you face them. God will allow you to run from the covenant, however, as he gives us that freedom to choose blessings or curses, life or death.

## The Difference between Covenant and Contract [2]

The idea of a contract is more familiar to us than the idea of a covenant, especially in Western society. Legal marriage comes from the idea of contract in that we enter into a contract with certain rights and responsibilities. A legal marriage can end in divorce. Contracts are based on conditions like "if you do this for me, I will do this for you." "If you don't meet my needs, then there will be a divorce." Covenant marriage, however, is not based on conditions of entitlement but on unconditional love and respect between two loving partners. Yes, at times that is difficult, especially in a ruptured relationship where there is very little connection. I will address this in a later chapter.

Here are some basic guidelines that covenant partners will find helpful in using contracts to build their relationships with each other:

- Do not mistake a contract for a covenant. Contracts should focus on helping us grow and deepen our relationship and resolve difficulties.
- Contracts are meant for positive change to create the environment of love and respect. An example of this could be, "I want you to spend one evening a week with me." Or, "I will take out the garbage during the week." In a relationship where a power struggle is present, a couple is rarely able to dialogue in adult-to-adult mode.
- Contracts are meant for specific requests. The acronym of PMS works here: P is for positive, what we want, not what we don't want. The M is for some measurement of time like over the next week. And the S means the request needs to be specific so that both parties know what it is.
- Make sure both partners are willing to make the marriage relationship the priority rather than what each individual partner wants. This is not an easy thing to accomplish in a society where the idea of entitlement dominates. Couples can have a radical positive change in their relationship when they begin to make the relationship the priority.

Why do couples need to have contracts? The point is that all couples have contracts with each other, whether they realize it or not. The question is whether they are healthy, adult-focused contracts, or unhealthy contracts that drag the marriage down.

## Nature of Covenant

Every significant and permanent intervention of God is formed into a covenant. In the fifteenth chapter of Genesis we find the covenant between God and Abraham. In verse eight, Abram said, "Lord God, how shall I know that I will inherit it?" (NKJV). God's answer was *covenant*. In other words, Abraham was looking for a sign from God as to his promise when the Lord said in verse five, "'Look now toward heaven, and count the stars if you are able to number them.' And He said to him, 'So shall your descendants be'" (NKJV). Can you imagine experiencing that? Here

# THE MYSTERY OF MARRIAGE COVENANT 31

is Abram looking at the number of the stars (literally billions), and God says to him, "So shall your descendents be." Remember that at that time, he was childless.

The word *covenant* in the Hebrew language is *beriyth* (ber-eeth'). It has the sense of cutting because at the time, God was setting the standard of covenant by making a passing between two severed pieces of flesh. This became the Jewish sacrifice. Jeremiah 34:18 states, "And I will give the men who have transgressed My covenant, who have not performed the words of the covenant which they made before Me, when they cut the calf in two and passed between the parts of it" (NKJV) The Greek word used in the New Testament is *diatheke*, meaning a covenant or testament.

The importance of Genesis 15:8–11 is that these verses present a picture of the coming new covenant in Christ.

> And he said, "Lord God, how shall I know that I will inherit it?" So He said to him, "Bring Me a three-year-old heifer, a three-year-old female goat, a three-year-old ram, a turtledove, and a young pigeon." Then he brought all these to Him and cut them in two, down the middle, and placed each piece opposite the other; but he did not cut the birds in two. And when the vultures came down on the carcasses, Abram drove them away (NKJV).

Verse nine reads, "So He said to him, 'Bring Me a three-year-old heifer, a three-year-old female goat, a three-year-old ram, a turtledove, and a young pigeon.'" Why did Abraham cut the calf, the goat, and the ram? To make a covenant, the animals had to be cut in two. The idea was that the same may be done to the one who breaks the covenant. A ruptured marriage relationship is, in fact, cut in two emotionally and spiritually. When our relationship with God is ruptured, the covenant between God and the individual is cut. Covenant requires a sacrifice. It requires a death, a life laid down. Covenant is made by passing through that death together into a new life.

Genesis 15:10-11 states, "Then he brought all these to Him and cut them in two, down the middle, and placed each piece opposite the other; but he did not cut the birds in two. And when the vultures came down on the carcasses, Abram drove them away." Abram's protecting the carcasses is no doubt symbolic of God making a covenant and leaving us with the responsibility of guarding the evidence of it. How? Through his Word.

Verse seventeen says, "And it came to pass, when the sun went down and it was dark, that behold, there appeared a smoking oven and a burning torch that passed between those pieces" (NKJV). Darkness, smoke, and fire mark the presence of God as it did at Mt. Sinai with Moses. Exodus 19:18 states, "Now Mount Sinai was completely in smoke, because the Lord descended upon it in fire. Its smoke ascended like the smoke of a furnace, and the whole mountain quaked greatly" (NKJV). In the midst of darkness, the Spirit of God kindled a torch and illuminated the animal pieces—the symbols of the covenant. The burning lamp can be seen as the emblem of divine Presence. When it is totally dark and there seems little hope, the Holy Spirit is there and will illuminate the evidence of God's covenant.

If only we could understand that revelation and truly become connected with the Father to grasp this truth. Only through connection with the Father do we allow the Holy Spirit to illuminate this hope when our life situation looks hopeless.

In the third verse of the third psalm, David called God "My glory and the One who lifts up my head" (NKJV). Jews were very demonstrative, and often when they saw a brother with his head down they would take his chin and lift it up. When God sees us discouraged, he will take our chins and lift them up. He will take the burden that is causing us to hang our heads and lift us up, no matter the situation. Through relationship with our Father through Jesus, we can be lifted up. That is the nature of the covenant we have with the Creator.

Apply this to covenant marriage. 1John 3:16 explains what unconditional love really is: "By this we know love, because He laid down His life for us. And we also ought to lay down our lives for the brethren" (NKJV). Hebrews 9:16–17 states, "For where there is a testament, there must also of necessity be the death of the testator. For a testament is in force after men are dead, since it has no power at all while the testator lives" (NKJV).

The first place in the Bible where blood is shed is in the third chapter of Genesis, after the fall. "Also for Adam and his wife the

Lord God made tunics of skin, and clothed them" (3:21 NKJV). At this time in the Bible, humans were vegetarians. God was covering the sin of Adam and Eve with blood by covering up the nakedness that brought them shame. Notice they did not have shame with their nakedness before the fall. This shedding of blood looked toward the scarlet thread throughout the Old Testament, pointing the way to Christ. So the covenant with Abram was significant with shedding of blood.

## The Kingdom of God Related to Blood Covenant

Blood covenant pointed the way to Christ. In the New Testament, in the week before his crucifixion, Jesus entered the gates of Jerusalem riding on a donkey, with the Jews welcoming him with palm branches. As the King rode on a donkey, on the other side of Jerusalem the sacrificial lambs—without spot or blemish—were entering the gates. These were the lambs to be used in a sacrificial offering, leading up to the priest going into the inner courts in the presence of God to atone for Israel's sins. Jesus was the sacrificial Lamb atoning of all of our sins, and this is the significance of blood covenant.

The Lord's Supper in Luke 22:14-20 reveals what led up to this event:

> When the hour had come, He sat down, and the twelve apostles with Him. Then He said to them, "With fervent desire I have desired to eat this Passover with you before I suffer; for I say to you, I will no longer eat of it until it is fulfilled in the kingdom of God." Then He took the cup, and gave thanks, and said, "Take this and divide it among yourselves; for I say to you, I will not drink of the fruit of the vine until the kingdom of God comes." And He took bread, gave thanks and broke it, and gave it to them, saying 'This is my body which is given for you; do this in remembrance of Me." Likewise He also took the cup after supper, saying, 'This cup is the new covenant in My blood, which is shed for you" (NKJV).

In a very important statement in this Scripture, Jesus said, "I will not drink of the fruit of the vine until the kingdom of God comes." On its own, we might not understand the significance of that statement. The

Bible is like treasure, and we can be thought of as the miners trying to unearth the riches within. When we read about this event in Jesus' life, we may be reminded of our experiences at a Communion service in church. Yet what happened after Jesus says this? He was arrested, tried, and then sent to his crucifixion.

The gospel of Mark states, "And they brought him to the place Golgotha, which is translated, Place of a Skull. Then they gave Him wine mingled with myrrh to drink, but He did not take it" (15: 22-23 NKJV). Jesus said he would not drink of the fruit of the vine until the kingdom of God came. He did not refuse because of the myrrh, but because it was wine—the fruit of the vine.

As Jesus was hanging on the cross, the Bible tells us that "After this, Jesus, knowing that all things were now accomplished, that the Scripture might be fulfilled, said, 'I thirst.' Now a vessel full of sour wine was sitting there; and they filled a sponge with sour wine, put it on hyssop, and put it to His mouth. So when Jesus had received the sour wine, He said, 'It is finished!' And bowing His head, He gave up His spirit" (John 19:28-30 NKJV).

It was at that moment that the kingdom of God came for us. The old covenant and the new covenant were fulfilled. "It is finished" meant the battle was over in Christ's life and in ours.

This is an incredible story of overcoming through the idea of blood covenant. In Revelation 3:21 Jesus says, "He who overcomes (is victorious), I will grant him to sit beside Me on My throne, as I Myself overcame (was victorious) and sat down beside My Father on His throne" (AMPLIFIED BIBLE).

Typically in a Communion service, a pastor might read Paul's account in 1 Corinthians 11:23-30, which reads this way:

> For I received from the Lord Himself that which I passed on to you [it was given to me personally], that the Lord Jesus on the night when He was treacherously delivered up and while His betrayal was in progress took bread, And when He had given thanks, He broke [it] and said, Take, eat. This is My body, which is broken for you. Do this to call Me [affectionately] to remembrance. Similarly when supper was ended, He took the cup also, saying, This cup is the new covenant [ratified and established] in My blood. Do this, as often as you drink [it], to call Me

# THE MYSTERY OF MARRIAGE COVENANT 35

[affectionately] to remembrance. For every time you eat this bread and drink this cup, you are representing and signifying and proclaiming the fact of the Lord's death until He comes [again]. So then whoever eats the bread or drinks the cup of the Lord in a way that is unworthy [of Him] will be guilty of [profaning and sinning against] the body and blood of the Lord. Let a man [thoroughly] examine himself, and [only when he has done] so should he eat of the bread and drink of the cup. For anyone who eats and drinks without discriminating and recognizing with due appreciation that [it is Christ's] body, eats and drinks a sentence (a verdict of judgment) upon himself. That [careless and unworthy participation] is the reason many of you are weak and sickly, and quite enough of you have fallen into the sleep of death (AMPLIFIED).

Verse twenty-seven says, "So then whoever eats the bread or drinks the cup of the Lord in a way that is unworthy [of Him] will be guilty of [profaning and sinning against] the body and blood of the Lord." For centuries we have been taught that to partake of Communion we need to be free of sin and repentant. In his second letter to the Corinthians, the apostle Paul says, "For though He was crucified in weakness, yet He lives by the power of God. For we also are weak in Him, but we shall live with Him by the power of God toward you. Examine yourselves *as to* whether you are in the faith. Test yourselves. Do you not know yourselves, that Jesus Christ is in you?—unless indeed you are disqualified" (13:4-5 NKJV). Combining Paul's account of Communion and this passage, we see that the reason many are weak and sick, and many sleep, is that we do not examine ourselves for who we are in Christ—who Christ is in our beings.

Jesus said "It is finished." That means our battle is over through blood covenant, and that he paid a price for our sins. If we see who we are in Christ and realize our potential through him, we position ourselves for blessings and favor. But if we do not examine who we are in Christ, we are unworthy to partake of the bread and the wine of Communion.

## First Hebrew Covenant Between Man

It is important to understand this idea of the new covenant that God made for us and with us, especially if we wish to begin understanding the significance of horizontal covenant with others—in particular with our spouse. The first example in the Bible of a horizontal covenant between two men is in First Samuel 18:1-5 with David and Jonathan. This example of a Hebrew covenant shows that it was meant to benefit both parties. They would come together before witnesses. In this beautiful story, Jonathan took off his robe, his armor, his sword, his bow, and his belt, and gave them to David. They were saying, "What is mine is yours, and what is yours is mine." The robe was especially significant because you could tell everything by a Jew's robe, including his wealth and his family. In giving David his robe, Jonathan gives everything he is and everything he has—every soldier, every army, and every weapon. He was saying, "Now we have one army."

Paul used a covenant expression in his letter to the Ephesians (4:22-24) when he talked about taking off the old man and putting on the new. After making the covenant with Jonathan, David prospered in all he did. The great love between David and Jonathan led to the covenant between them.

The Abrahamic covenant includes changing names: from Abram to Abraham, and from Sari to Sarah. Our marriage ceremonies developed from these covenant ideas, and these principles have been in effect for thousands of years. But we see in contemporary history an almost complete breakdown of covenant principles. Even the principle of name changes when the wife takes her husband's name is challenged by the feminist movement. Covenant is not about selfishness. It is about giving and receiving. The breakdown of marriages can be directly tracked to the loss of commitment to marriage vows and the lack of understanding of the covenant relationship.

We are self-oriented. The contemporary attitude in Western society is "What can I get?" We live in a selfish culture that programs us from the time we are born all the way through adulthood. But any relationship based on this notion will be a disaster. Instead, a healthy marriage or relationship needs to be based not on "What can I get?" but rather on, "What can I give? Will I lay down my life for my partner?"

## The Biblical Notion of Covenant is Vertical and Horizontal

We can have two types of covenants. A horizontal covenant is between people. An example from the Old Testament would be the covenant between David and Jonathan. A vertical covenant is between God and his people. The covenant God made with Abraham is an example of this.

> The cup of blessing which we bless, is it not the communion of the blood of Christ? The bread which we break, is it not the communion of the body of Christ? For we, though many, are one bread and one body; for we all partake of that one bread.
> —1 Cor. 10:16–17 NKJV

A horizontal relationship is emphasized between all who partake of the one loaf and the one cup.

> But you *are* a chosen generation, a royal priesthood, a holy nation, His own special people, that you may proclaim the praises of Him who called you out of darkness into His marvelous light; who once *were* not a people but *are* now the people of God, who had not obtained mercy but now have obtained mercy.
> —1 Pet. 2:9-10 NKJV

This passage declares that the new covenant in Christ has the same effect as God's previous covenant with Israel. It established all who enter into it as a "collective people."

The purpose of the marriage covenant is to bring a man and a woman into union with each other. This principle applies with equal force to the third case: the covenant between Christian believers. The purpose is to bring Christians into union with each other. Unfortunately, we will have few horizontal covenant relationships in our lifetime. In Exodus chapters twenty through twenty-three, where we read of God making his covenant with Israel at Mt. Sinai, he immediately explained to the Israelites the obligations that the covenant would impose on their relationships.

## The Qualities of a Covenant Marriage[3]

The love of God for his people is difficult to understand with the "natural" mind. God is a Spirit and only our spiritual mind can truly understand his unconditional love. When the Old and New Testament writers wanted an illustration to describe that supernatural love, they often used a picture of the marriage relationship. In Ephesians 5:21–30, Paul gives us an image of the relationship between husband and wife to describe the bride and bridegroom. The bridegroom is Jesus, and the bride is the body of Christ, the church. Paul tells husbands "love your wives, just as Christ also loved the church and gave Himself for her, that He might sanctify and cleanse her with the washing of water by the word, that He might present her to Himself a glorious church, not having spot or wrinkle or any such thing, but that she should be holy and without blemish" (5:25-27 NKJV).

A marriage relationship can demonstrate God's relationship with us only if that marriage truly mirrors Christ's love for us. If we examine God's covenant with those he loves, this can give us guidance for living in the covenant of marriage. This is a wonderful ideal, but so often the church does not help us understand how to develop that type of love.

## Covenant Marriage was not meant to be Temporary

Lamentations 3:22 tells us that God's love and compassion never fails: "Because of the LORD's great love we are not consumed, for his compassions never fail" (NIV). Romans 8:38–39 tells us that nothing, "neither death nor life, neither angels nor demons, neither the present nor the future, nor any powers, neither height nor depth, nor anything else in all creation, will be able to separate us from the love of God that is in Christ Jesus our Lord" (NIV). God's love is patient and enduring, even though hurt and disappointment touch our lives. The essence of a covenant is that it is unconditional.

## There is a Cost to Covenant Marriage

The book of Exodus tells us the Israelites walked away from the gods the Egyptians worshipped and followed God to wander in the wilderness. They gave up tables of food and security for an uncertain future with God. I cannot even imagine how frightening that must have been and it was no wonder that their faith was tested. The text reads, "In the desert the whole community grumbled against Moses and Aaron. The Israelites said to them, 'If only we had died by the LORD's hand in Egypt! There we sat around pots of meat and ate all the food we wanted, but you have brought us out into this desert to starve this entire assembly to death'" (16:2-3 NIV).

The marriage covenant, like a blood covenant which is described earlier in this chapter, requires a death—a giving up of the life we know for an uncertain future of commitment to each other. Without the understanding of the concept of covenant, most Americans haven't a clue what a marriage covenant means. In the biblical time of the Judges, when Ruth entered into a covenant with Naomi, it required she uproot herself out of her comfort zone and go to a new and strange place. We go through similar issues when we enter into covenant marriage. This also requires a foundation of faith.

Romans 12:3 states, "For I say, through the grace given to me, to everyone who is among you, not to think of himself more highly than he ought to think, but to think soberly, as God has dealt to each one a measure of faith" (NKJV). That means all who know Jesus as our Savior have the same measure, or amount, of faith. While it would appear that some individuals in the body of Christ have more faith than others, that is only because they have learned how to activate the faith that is already there.

There is both an individuality of freedom and an obligation to our partner in covenant marriage. Although we have a responsibility in a covenant marriage, we cannot force the other person to live up to that commitment. We have to allow them the freedom to change. God has given us the right to have a free will. He will not force us to go where we are not willing to go. Above all, covenant marriage is about being relational. Listening to each other is the key, along with the principle of "intentionality," two subjects we will discuss in later sections of the book.

Diana Richmond Garland mentioned the promises of covenant marriage in *Covenant Marriage*.[4] A true covenant relationship with a spouse is going to be grounded in unconditional love as in 1 Corinthians 13. The covenant marriage is going to be grounded in a walk of forgiveness for any wrong or hurt given or received, such as in Ephesians 4:32: "And be kind to one another, tenderhearted, forgiving one another, even as God in Christ forgave you" (NKJV).

The individuals in a covenant marriage should be able to feel safe and comforted by knowing they will be heard by their partner rather than being given unsolicited advice or an "I told you so." A couple in a covenant marriage should foster an atmosphere of hope by focusing on the positives of what can be done rather than what cannot be done. They should see their differences as sources of strength rather than sources of conflict. My wife has been so supportive in my profession of helping couples, and I don't know if I could have done this without her support. That sense of support and secure attachment with each other is what a covenant marriage should foster.

Perhaps you are at the place where you long to have—or to restore—the covenant in your marriage. Keep in mind that our God does impossible things in impossible situations. If you are at this point, have hope and make a decision to activate the words below in your own life.

## Point of Decision

First there is a commitment to God—your personal relationship with God. Once you have prayed that commitment, do not begin to reason or speculate. You will not understand God in the natural, but only in the spirit. So begin to cultivate that spiritual relationship.

Next, if you are ready, there is your commitment to your partner. That commitment will take patience and intentionality. If you are not yet ready for this commitment, seek counseling from a qualified professional Christian counselor who specializes in marriages or relationships. Ideally, you and your mate should commit to this counseling at the same time. But sometimes one party is ready before the other. Just as Christ awaits our readiness to accept him as our Savior, understand and accept your mate's position.

Make your commitment now and trust God to bring your mate to this same position. State that commitment out loud and maintain your commitment—even if you see no evidence of change. God often is working behind the scenes.

Try to not go by what you feel, what you see, and what you think. Instead, try to go by the Word of God and his promises. Remember, we have free will to walk away from God or toward him.

*Chapter Three*

# AH! YOUNG LOVE: THERE'S BANANA SPLITS, THEN SPLITTING OF ASSETS

> When it gets really bad, that's when it's about to change; and most people leave when it's really bad, so they never get to the changes, and I think that is such a tragedy!
> —Harville Hendrix

GEORGE BERNARD SHAW once described marriage as an institution that brings together two people "under the influence of the most violent, most insane, most delusive, and most transient of passions. They are required to swear that they will remain in that excited, abnormal, and exhausting condition until death do them part." One of Shaw's contemporaries, journalist and social reformer Jacob Riis, wrote, "When nothing seems to help, I go and look at a stonecutter hammering away at his rock perhaps a hundred times without as much as a crack showing in it. Yet at the hundred and first blow it will split in two, and I know it was not that blow that did it—but all that had gone before."

On a Friday night several decades ago, while attending a single's ministry at a church in Orlando, Florida, my life changed forever when I saw Susan for the first time. This weekly event was a night to look forward to when I was single and did not want to go into bars to find companionship and fellowship. That night at church I turned my head and saw a beautiful woman enter the room. I couldn't help notice her long blonde hair and hourglass figure. She looked like a movie star. (Of course at church we aren't supposed to notice things like the hot pink pants she wore.) But rather than face the possibility of rejection, I didn't make any contact with her that night.

Thinking about her the next day, I realized I had seen her years before at an Aglow meeting in Orlando where I was singing. I recall seeing her in the back of the room when I was on the platform. (I would later find out her mother had been with her.) That same weekend, I saw her and her two beautiful daughters climb out of a sporty 280Z in the parking lot of a church I was visiting. At that point, I dismissed her, assuming she was married. A couple of years later, God was still at work. When a mutual friend introduced us, I discovered she was not married.

When I look back on those days, as a deep romantic love began, I realize that at the time I didn't have a good understanding of what romantic love even looked like. That understanding didn't come until my therapist handed me a book called *Getting the Love You Want*, by Harville Hendrix. This was when Susan and I were separated and I did not know how we could have been so in love one day and mortal enemies the next. It took me longer than it should have to understand the problems that led to our downfall.

As I read Hendrix's book I started beginning to understand what a godly romantic relationship was supposed to look like. Answers came slowly, partially because of my own stubbornness. It felt like trying to swim upstream against a rushing current, but I kept on paddling by being intentional.

## Healing Through Self-Awareness

The first step of therapeutic healing comes through self-awareness. The idea is to know where we are in our environments in life, which includes the awareness of who we are in our relationships. This concept reminded me of my Ranger training in the Army during the Vietnam War. We had to learn to be aware of our environment or we would most likely die.

In relationships, we also need to learn to be self aware of whether we are connecting or disconnecting. Imagine that I am sitting in our family room drinking a cup of coffee and enjoying the morning solitude. From behind my chair I hear my wife walk into the kitchen. I hear her take a

# AH! YOUNG LOVE: THERE'S BANANA SPLITS, THEN SPLITTING OF ASSETS

seat in our breakfast area, which overlooks our backyard garden as she prepares a light breakfast of toasted Ezekiel bread. If my self-awareness is at a high point, I will realize I should go sit with her and connect by sharing our day. That connection behavior will mean something to her. But if I just sit drinking my coffee, I will send the message that I am oblivious to her presence. The idea is to decrease disconnection and increase connection. I've learned that Susan inevitably appreciates those connections before we start the day.

I have worked with couples, especially the men, who have the same struggle I did with understanding what a romantic relationship looks like. Unfortunately, much of our programming regarding romantic love comes from movies and television. When is the last time you saw a movie about a married couple who had been together for decades? *Golden Pond* in the 1980s comes to mind. To understand what romantic love truly is, we need to look at history.

As romantic love has played a more prevalent role in mate selection, and our society has become more dysfunctional from broken homes, the first step in understanding needs to be education on romantic relationships. This includes understanding the scriptural significance God intended through marriage covenant, which we examined in the previous chapter. The other aspect is the more practical application of living out the emotional part of relationships.

## Our Position in Christ

The second step is learning more about ourselves. One aspect of this is to learn who we are "in Christ"—and what God's purpose is for us. As we get in touch with ourselves and free our natural man to become more of what God intends, we will allow our spirit man to rise and dominate our natural man. That comes from connecting with God and going to the next level in our relationship with him. At that point we will become the individual God intends, which means we can then become the partner in marriage that we are intended to be.

In a later chapter we will discuss how to overcome fear of failure and fear of people—two things that will stop us from reaching our dreams in our lives and relationships.

## Healthy Relationship Training

The third step is to begin learning and training ourselves in the skills of a healthy relationship. In no other area has the church fallen so short. Most of us know the Scriptures about what we are to do in our marriages. But somebody please tell us how to do that! Most Christian literature on this subject is more of an ideal for marriages that are already in good shape. A marriage in crisis, however, needs a deeper experience. This may be why the divorce rate in the church recently surpassed that of the world. We need to go to a deeper level in understanding the emotional part of relationships.

This is an area where church leadership often fails. Too many pastors are trying to build their own kingdom instead of God's kingdom. If the church is to serve as a model for people in the world, I do not understand why we fail to focus on marriages. The church is about relationships. The godly marriage is the model of the ultimate bride and groom—the church (the bride) and Jesus Christ (the groom). If we would focus on getting our act together in marriages, the world would want what we have—an eternal life with our heavenly Father. The Spirit of Christ is what draws those outside of a relationship with God to him.

Personally and professionally, I believe that Imago Relationship Therapy contains all the concepts we need to achieve a godly marriage. It is the dream of some Imago therapists to take that experience into churches of all denominations.

## Cutting the Cord on Your Baggage

The fourth step is to begin healing the defensive structures we have built, and learning how to change our behaviors to meet the needs of our partner. This requires a journey of learning and change, and this kind of change takes time because healing usually comes in baby steps. While God could heal us in a second, he seems to want our participation in that healing. Part of that journey of learning and change means developing a deeper relationship with God through his Word, spending time in prayer, and listening to the voice of the Holy Spirit. The other part of that journey involves dealing with family-of-origin issues that affect us as adults. We will learn more about this in another chapter.

## The Stages of Love as Applied to Mate Selection: Romance, Disconnection, Vintage Love

How and why does something that starts out feeling so good go downhill after taking that step of marriage commitment? If we don't understand the stages of love, we could walk away from the love of our life. Most couples break up right before the breakthrough.

The greatest problem in our society does not come from drugs, alcohol, or a lack of prayer in school. The key problem is broken marriages. The most sacred example God intends as a model for the body of Christ has come dangerously close to extinction, for the godly idea of covenant marriage is being attacked from every direction. We are the victims of centuries of failed parenting and loveless marriages. By loveless marriages I am referring to arranged marriages—ones where love and romance were not controlling factors in the relationship, but rather a sense of duty.

I believe the generational curse we talk about so often in Christian circles is an emotional curse passed down from generation to generation. In psychology circles, this is known as "family-of-origin issues." In biblical terms, the sins of the fathers are passed down to the third and fourth generation. However we want to refer to this issue, it is an important area that couples need to work on to create empathy, understanding, and healing in their relationships.

Humankind is the very apex of God's creative work, originally intended to commune with him, as was the case with Adam and Eve. The human mind and emotions is the point at which nature has become conscious of self. We are the only species with the ability to reason, yet we are also the most wounded. God's nature is trying to heal itself through healed relationships.

The agenda of Christianity is to heal relationships through and with God—and then to heal others. Verses twenty-one and twenty-two of Romans chapter eight state that "the creation itself also will be delivered from the bondage of corruption into the glorious liberty of the children of God. For we know that the whole creation groans and labors with birth pangs together until now" (NKJV). Healing begins through our salvation in Jesus Christ, which is a relational healing, and through the healing of our marriages, which leads to healed families.

In *Getting the Love You Want,* Harville Hendrix describes the stages of love.[1] He writes that romantic love has not always been involved in mate selection. In fact, it is a recent phenomenon in history. Down through the millennia, marriages were arranged, beginning with the marriage of Adam and Eve. Rarely was romantic love involved in mate selection. It was, however, usually involved with adulterous affairs or relationships outside of marriage. Marriages were arranged by an authority in a society or by parents. Ancient Greek scholars, around the fifth century before Christ, began exploring the notion of individual rights, but it took a very long time before these concepts would influence mate selection in marriages.

Only gradually did Western culture begin to evolve to the state of democracy. That began around the 1600s when scholars started studying ancient Greek philosophies. This eventually led to such events as the Separatists coming to New England and putting into practice the early concepts of a free society. Many of their ideas led early Americans to declare independence from England, and they also were responsible for deep changes within many European countries. With ideas of democracy came the concepts of freedom and self-ownership.

Beginning in the nineteenth century—and picking up steam in the twentieth century—there was a gradual change away from arranged marriages to the notion of romantic love in mate selection. Among the greatest influences promoting this idea in the twentieth century were movies and television. Our society has come to accept the notion of love as portrayed metaphorically by two people running in slow motion across a meadow, embracing in the middle, and seeing skyrockets go off. As long as this euphoric feeling exists, the couple must be in love. And when it doesn't exist, they are obviously with the wrong partner. So say movies and television.

What was really going on in Western culture was that for the first time in history, the attraction between men and women was directed into and contained within the structure of marriage. When our culture was based on arranged marriages, ones designed so the partners would survive their environmental struggles, the divorce rate was low. But when romantic love became the driving force in mate selection, and when the experience of early love faded, confusion would set in and couples started questioning whether they were in the right marriage. And of course that led to a steep climb in the divorce rate.

Divorce did not appear on the scene in really large numbers until the emotional upheaval of World War II. After men came home from the war, divorce gradually became a standard option for relationship problems. We began to just walk away from the problem—not realizing we were just carrying the same problem to another relationship. Yet most couples do not want divorce; they want an end to the pain. If they could find the way to heal the pain, many marriages could be saved.

So let us begin looking at the three stages of love and how we can navigate through them. Even when we are aware of these stages, we have a tough time applying this information to our own situations. The first question is, Are we really falling in love when we first feel that attraction to someone else? Usually we are not actually falling in love, but instead, as the honeymoon stage of love will describe, falling in lust. Real love begins when the honeymoon stage, or infatuation stage, ends. Author John Bradshaw calls that stage "the post romantic stress syndrome."

## The Honeymoon Stage of Love: "You Make Me Feel Brand New"

The honeymoon stage of love involves what has become known as romantic love. When we are in this stage, we want the feeling to last forever. In fact, we expect it to last forever. This stage begins with an attraction to a person which could happen gradually over time, or even lead to "love at first sight" when we catch a glimpse of someone across the room and our knees become weak as the attraction process takes hold. The group called The Stylistics captured this kind of feeling in their 1970s hit "You Make Me Feel Brand New." The song describes the wonder people experience at the beginning of a new love.

Why doesn't this magical state of love last? How can we feel so brand new at first, only to realize later that this same person drives us crazy? I have seen over a thousand couples in my marriage counseling practice. Most began with this honeymoon stage of their brand new love, and then eventually their relationship went into a downward spiral. I have seen this so often I am led to believe that perhaps this passionate stage of love was never meant to last indefinitely, but instead it was meant to bring two incompatible people together to be healed. It fascinates me that science can often mesh with the concepts God has revealed in the Scriptures. When this happens, one can see the wisdom of God in the Bible rather than a purely legalistic approach.

Attraction operates in three areas: physical, psychological, and social. We are attracted to a person's spirituality, their athletic ability, their morals, their spontaneity, their approach to their family, their smile, their eyes, their body—the list could go on and on. The physical area of attraction seems to involve symmetry, which we unconsciously associate with health and fertility. There is a certain look or figure that we become attracted to. When we see someone with this look, it is hard for us to take our eyes off them.

The psychological area encompasses the emotional perspective. As we so often hear, opposites do seem to attract, perhaps even more than we suspect. Some research suggests that we are attracted to a person with DNA least like our own. The way the person presents himself or herself can seem familiar. What we don't realize at this stage is that we are being attracted to a person who quite possibly could drive us crazy.

The social idea of attraction is that many men want a trophy, and many women look for security. Think, for example, of older celebrities with younger women. For those women, being with an older man means financial security. The idea that women want financial security and men look for a trophy does not depend on one's economical scale. Beauty is in the eyes of the beholder, so a trophy to one may not be a trophy to another. Some women are not looking for security financially, as they have a career that provides that. The best way I can summarize this idea is to quote the old saying that "for every pot there is a lid to fit it."

Psychologists tell us that we are attracted to both the positive and negative traits of our caretakers. John Money, a sexologist, calls this mechanism "love maps," which are templates with brain circuitry that determine what arouses us sexually, and what drives us to fall in love with one person rather than another.

In *The Anatomy of Love*, anthropologist Helen Fisher, interacts with John Money's ideas. She writes, "As you grow up, this unconscious map takes shape and a composite proto-image of the ideal sweetheart

## AH! YOUNG LOVE: THERE'S BANANA SPLITS, THEN SPLITTING OF ASSETS

gradually emerges. You have a mental picture of your perfect mate, the settings you find enticing, and the kinds of conversations and erotic activities that excite you." Harville Hendrix calls this the *Imago,* which comes from a Latin word for image. The idea is the same.

As we develop as children, we begin to get an image or love map of what a husband and wife, or a father and mother should be. Our caretakers become models for us as we develop emotionally, and this model is imprinted into our brain. As we grow into adulthood, this unconscious Imago begins taking shape and becomes an image of what we look for in the ideal lover. When we see individuals who fit these patterns, it triggers that attraction, which tells us that we have to be with that person. I once heard author John Bradshaw say that if you feel this with someone, run for the exit as fast as you can, because you are about to enter a danger zone.

As we become attracted to an individual and begin a love relationship, we enter into a stage of romantic love that sometimes will drive us crazy. This phase is called "infatuation." Infatuation is being carried away by our feelings to such a point that one lacks sound judgment. Some researchers call this nature's drive to perpetuate the species. Author John Bradshaw calls this stage the beginning of the "post romantic stress disorder." He says we do not fall in love so much as fall in *lust,* and that true love begins when infatuation ends. In the 1980s and 1990s, investigators began looking into what happens when we fall in love, or hit the limerence (limbo) state. Through MRI research of the brain, it was revealed that when we enter the infatuation stage we are on an adrenaline rush, with the release of natural narcotics into our bloodstream.

In *The Truth About Love,* Pat Love calls this rush a "love cocktail." This mixture contains dopamine, nor epinephrine, and phenyl ethylamine. Phenyl ethylamine (PEA) is known as the "passion drug" because it gives the feeling of high passion during this altered state of consciousness. It has properties that include creating euphoria or ecstasy, a lowering of defenses, a positive outlook, being energized, and having an increased libido or sexual desire, enhanced by danger, fear, and risk.

There is evidence that love is primitive and that infatuation and attachment are very old emotions, according to psychiatrist Michael Liebowitz. He theorizes that the euphoria and energy of attraction are caused by a brain bath of naturally occurring amphetamines that pool in the emotional centers of the brain. He says this is why infatuated lovers can stay awake all night talking, why they become so optimistic, so gregarious, and so full of life. What they are experiencing is an altered state of consciousness. This is why affairs are so dangerous. People having an affair compare their altered state of consciousness to the pain of their present relationship. What they don't realize is that the altered state will lose the feeling of high passion and become what they are presently in pain about.

During this altered state of consciousness, we are not our normal selves. If we don't talk much, we talk all the time; if we don't like our jobs, we tend to thrive at them. Our friends usually think we have disappeared. If we don't like sex, we cannot keep our hands off each other. For people during this stage, I turn to the wisdom of God. As the creator of our bodies, he knows that during this infatuation state of increased libido when we have sex with a partner, a flood of oxytocin is released into our bodies, which gives us the tremendous bonding we feel during orgasm. God does not want us to have sex outside of marriage because, in his infinite wisdom, he knows we could be bonded to a person we are not supposed to marry—or even be in a relationship with. Abstinence is the key to preventing this.

Oxytocin is released at three different occasions: during childbirth, as oxytocin seems to aid loss of the memory of the pain the mother experiences, when a mother nurses her baby, and during the sexual act. This is why it is so important to teach our kids abstinence and why singles need to practice it. Many mistaken marriages have been created through premarital sex because individuals bonded with the wrong person.

I am not advocating that one should heap guilt upon himself or herself if they have had premarital sex. And I am not advocating that anyone should get a divorce if they had premarital sex before marriage. What I am advocating is repentance for moral failures. Repentance means going to God and asking for forgiveness, and then turning from our way to his way. It means seeking divine guidance and trusting that God does forgive us.

During this infatuation stage of love, couples usually make their relationship and one another's needs a priority. They laugh and play with each other and usually work out difficulties while also accepting

# AH! YOUNG LOVE: THERE'S BANANA SPLITS, THEN SPLITTING OF ASSETS

each other's differences. They flirt and connect with each other. Little do most suspect that they have been attracted to a person who, later in the relationship, will drive each other crazy. Research psychiatrist Liebowitz says this revved up level of excitement was never intended to last because the brain could not sustain it over a lifetime.

Science is not certain what happens as lovers move out of this altered state. Either our body adjusts to the natural narcotics being released into the body, or the brain stops sending the signal to release them as we move through infatuation and on to the attachment stage of romantic love. Liebowitz' research shows that at this stage, with the excitement and novelty subsiding, the brain kicks in new chemicals, the endorphins—natural morphine-like substances that calm the mind. Helen Fisher, in her book *Anatomy of Love*, writes about this occurrence. She writes that Liebowitz says that as the endorphins surge along the brain's primeval pathways, they usher in this "attachment" stage of love with its sensations of security and peace. It appears that an insecurely-attached person falls more deeply in love, while securely attached individuals know how to get their needs met.

We do not look for a person to fall in love with, but rather we look for a person who can meet our needs. Many individuals are looking for the right person to love rather than trying to become the right person.

When we are in the attachment stage of romantic love, we continue courting by touching, holding, gazing, listening, responding, supporting, and honoring one another. Healthy attachment behaviors produce an endorphin response which leaves us calm, safe, secure, confident, and comforted. All human beings are inherently driven toward attachment or an enduring affection bond. John Bolby, an English psychiatrist who developed attachment theory in relationships, says that "human beings of all ages are found to be at their happiest and to be able to deploy their talents to best advantage when they are confident that, standing behind them, there is one or more trusted persons who will come to their aid should difficulties arise."

When we don't feel that attachment—or when there is a lack of an attachment figure during a relationship—this produces a protest leading to despair and then detachment. This leads to the next stage of love—the impasse or disconnection stage.

Anthropologist Helen Fisher describes in her book, *The Anatomy of Love,* this two-phase progression of romance, saying, "When two people are first together, their hearts are on fire and their passion is very great. After a while, the fire cools and that's how it stays. They continue to love each other, but it's in a different way—warm and dependable." What is remarkable, Fisher has found in her research, is that the vast majority of people acknowledge that romantic passion exists. She states that "a new study of 168 societies found that eighty-seven percent of these vastly different cultures displayed direct evidence that people knew this madness."

The beliefs of the *honeymoon stage* are that "Everything is right with the world," "Love will conquer all," "You are the one for me," and "If you leave me I'll die."

## The Disconnection Stage of Love: "You Don't Bring Me Flowers Anymore"

After the romantic stage of love, which can last anywhere from six months to two years, couples gradually move toward disconnection. One of the biggest illusions in our culture is that the honeymoon stage will last forever, that is, if you just find the right partner. We begin discovering this disconnection stage through disappointment with our partner. Disappointment leads to disillusionment, which leads to coercion, and then to an impasse.

Years ago, Neil Diamond and Barbara Streisand sang "You Don't Bring Me Flowers Anymore," which tells the story of a couple disconnecting. The first line basically says it all: "You don't bring me flowers; you don't sing me love songs." It is difficult to understand how someone with whom we could have been so in love—a relationship that made us feel "brand new"—could get to the place where "you don't bring me flowers anymore." Yet all is not lost. We can learn how to have that dream relationship if we are willing to work to find it. Remember, couples don't want divorce, they want an end to pain.

The individual who is "anxiously attached" will appear as clinging, and they will have difficulty with separation from their partner. They will need consistent contact, and they will tend to idealize their partners.

# AH! YOUNG LOVE: THERE'S BANANA SPLITS, THEN SPLITTING OF ASSETS

To prevent separation, they will overlook their partner's faults. An avoidantly attached individual will attach to objects and work, will be uncomfortable in social situations, and will tend to withdraw and become defensive.

This state of impasse leads to a disconnect from the person with whom, during the honeymoon stage, they were so in love. This is the point where the couple could decide to leave each other through separation or divorce. The problem with leaving the relationship is that we eventually meet someone else and start the whole process all over again. Either that, or the relationship evolves into an *invisible divorce* where the couple stays in a passionless marriage for the sake of the kids, church, or family. Neither is the will of God, for the Father reveals in Deuteronomy, "I call heaven and earth as witnesses today against you, that I have set before you life and death, blessing and cursing; therefore choose life, that both you and your descendants may live" (30:19 NKJV). Leaving one problem to enter into another is choosing curses, not blessings.

I believe that after we fall in love and as we move out of that limerence or limbo state, we begin to see the negatives we could not see before. It is almost as if the "love cocktail" blindfolds us so we are not aware of these negatives. Perhaps we are aware of them below the surface, but we do not want to acknowledge them. After a while the negatives become overwhelming. Most of the positive traits are still there, but we just cannot see them. That is why we can act in a completely different way towards others outside the relationship. We don't live with them.

In the disconnection stage of love there is often a conflict about issues like control, neatness, doing one's part, closeness or other space issues, and feeling unimportant or alone. During a conflict, the danger signs gradually begin appearing, such as the need to always be right.

Marriage researcher John Gottman calls these danger signs the "four horsemen of the apocalypse." They are criticism, defensiveness, contempt, and stonewalling. Through more than twenty years of research into what makes marriages work, Gottman has developed a way to predict, with ninety-three percent accuracy, a couple's potential of getting divorced. He does this by hearing how they deal with conflict. When he hears communication styles using the four horsemen, he knows the relationship is on rocky ground if something doesn't change.

Actually, the disconnection stage is the greatest opportunity to grow into the individuals God wants us to become. Harville Hendrix states that "conflict is growth trying to happen." If we can learn to meet our partner's needs—the way they need them met and not the way we think they need them met—then we can have the dream relationship we have longed for. Whereas the Golden Rule tells us to "do unto others as you would have them do unto you," the Imago Relationship community prefers to use what it calls the Platinum Rule. It states, "Do unto others as they need to have done unto them."

The message we send in the honeymoon stage is, "if you leave me I will die." The message we send in the disconnect stage is "if you don't leave me, I'll kill you." The real answer is to evolve to the third stage of love, which is unconditional love.

## The Transformation Stage: "Buy Me a Rose"

To move from the disconnect stage of relationship love to a safer and more passionate relationship requires a transformation process. In Romans 12:2 the apostle Paul states, "And do not be conformed to this world, but be transformed by the renewing of your mind, that you may prove what is that good and acceptable and perfect will of God" (NKJV). We need a renewed mind to begin to understand what has caused the relationship to disconnect. We need to move from blame, shame, and guilt to understanding how to heal the relationship through compassion and empathy. The process of transformation comes through acquiring information and learning skills and processes to begin growing into the relationship of our dreams.

This transformation is depicted in a song by Kenny Rogers, "Buy Me a Rose." This ballad tells of a husband trying to please his wife with material objects, such as a "three-car garage and her own credit cards." But this does not satisfy the wife. She wants simpler things, such as being bought a rose. Rogers says this song has brought him many letters from couples whose marriage has been healed.

# AH! YOUNG LOVE: THERE'S BANANA SPLITS, THEN SPLITTING OF ASSETS

## The Unconditional Love or Vintage Love Stage: "Through the Years"

There is only one person who walked this earth knowing how to naturally love unconditionally. That person was Jesus Christ. We know how to fall in love and how to fight, as we are born with that ability. We don't, however, know how to love unconditionally in a natural way. We have to learn how to do that. 1 Peter 3:8– 9 states, "Finally, all of you be of one mind, having compassion for one another; love as brothers, be tenderhearted, be courteous; not returning evil for evil or reviling for reviling, but on the contrary blessing, knowing that you were called to this, that you may inherit a blessing" (NKJV). Romans 12:2 says, "And do not be conformed to this world, but be transformed by the renewing of your mind, that you may prove what is that good and acceptable and perfect will of God" (NKJV).

To learn how to love unconditionally requires a transformation process by the renewing of our minds. I define a couple's unconditional love in this stage as honoring, valuing, respecting, trusting, and listening. When we are walking in that type of relationship, we will be in a safe, passionate place—as God intends. We have to learn how to honor, value, respect, trust, and listen to each other. We are not naturally equipped to do this because we are all, to some degree, self-absorbed. We live in a self-oriented society, and our internal dialogue has been programmed from birth. We all fall short of the glory of God. We are not perfect, so why should we act like we are?

To guard against this, we might ask ourselves:

- Am I honoring my partner? How?
- Am I showing that I value my partner? How?
- Am I showing respect toward my partner? How?
- Am I developing a trusting relationship with my partner?
- Am I truly listening to my partner?

If someone were looking at your relationship, what evidence would they see that true love exists? Probably the single most important thing that keeps couples from transforming from the disconnection stage to the stage of unconditional love is a lack of empathy toward each other. Actually, it is this lack of empathy that causes the disconnection.

Empathy between partners means being able to understand how our partner feels when we hurt them or make them angry. When this ability fades, the emotional safety also fades between the couple and distance begins to develop. When that distance develops, relational intimacy almost always disappears. Many couples come to my office wanting renewed intimacy in their relationship, or to restore the sexuality they once enjoyed. Usually they begin to understand that until they feel safe with each other emotionally, it will be difficult to restore the intimacy they had in the honeymoon stage. Think of empathy as the glue that keeps couples connected.

Another trait that will keep us from developing the relationship of our dreams is our lack of *intentionality.* No matter how much therapy we undergo, or how many books we read, or how many sermons we hear on great marriages, if we are not intentional about reaching our dream, it will not happen, period. I see this all the time in my office, and it still amazes me. A couple will invest their time and money in marriage counseling, but they will be intentional only in the context of the counseling session. They will not take anything they learn in the session and implement it in their relationship outside of counseling. If we want to succeed, we have to be intentional.

One way to create those new habits is to get index cards and write statements of intentionality on them. One I use says "Do it now." I often tell couples to get a vision of the relationship they want, develop a burning desire to reach that dream no matter the pain, and then refuse to micromanage the journey. Be intentional about the vision. Another way is to *become self-aware.* That means becoming aware of where I am in my environment: driving a car, in my career, in my social awareness, and especially in my relationship with my wife.

As Christians, we really have no choice whether or not we should learn to love our partners unconditionally. If we are truly walking with God, that is his only commandment to us:

> Beloved, let us love one another, for love is of God; and everyone who loves is born of God and knows God. He who does not love does not

# AH! YOUNG LOVE: THERE'S BANANA SPLITS, THEN SPLITTING OF ASSETS

> know God, for God is love. In this the love of God was manifested toward us, that God has sent His only begotten Son into the world, that we might live through Him. In this is love, not that we loved God, but that He loved us and sent His Son to be the propitiation for our sins. Beloved, if God so loved us, we also ought to love one another. No one has seen God at any time. If we love one another, God abides in us, and His love has been perfected in us. By this we know that we abide in Him, and He in us, because He has given us of His Spirit.
> —1 John 4:7–13 NKJV

This is not a legalistic statement, but a scriptural principle. The fact is that we cannot proclaim to love God and not love one another. As Dr. Phil states, "We have to earn our way out of this marriage." Just because it is a little tough does not give us the right to walk away from our partner—not if we still want to proclaim to love God. It just does not fit.

Shania Twain has recorded a song called "From This Moment On," which has become a favorite at many weddings. When we get married, we do tend to think the moment we are in will last forever. The thoughts that flood our minds as we exchange our wedding vows can be revived in this third stage of real, unconditional love. When we reclaim this relationship, it is a deep and safe one filled with passion. It does not depend on the "love cocktail" that brought us together to meet, mate, and procreate. We can have a new relationship that begins "from this moment on," a relationship where the priority is to stay connected while we still have a sense of our individuality.

My experience in my own marriage leads me to believe that as we journey into healing, we experience a memory loss. We remember the painful events, but not the feelings of pain. You would have to reach this unconditional or vintage love stage to understand this phenomenon.

*Chapter Four*
---

# LIPOSUCTION OF YOUR SOUL—YOUR MIND, EMOTIONS, AND WILL

**What is a stronghold? Anything that has a strong hold on you!**

> For though we live in the world, we do not wage war as the world does. The weapons we fight with are not the weapons of the world. On the contrary, they have divine power to demolish strongholds. We demolish arguments and every pretension that sets itself up against the knowledge of God, and we take captive every thought to make it obedient to Christ. And we will be ready to punish every act of disobedience, once your obedience is complete.
> —2 Cor. 10:3-6 NIV

RAIN PELTED MY uncle's house in Fairmont, West Virginia, as I stood on the front porch. Tears streaked down my little boy's face as my mother left me for the first time in my life. I was slightly less than three years old, and it was a traumatic experience. To understand this scene, I need to take you back to my birth in Sanford, Florida. It was during World War II, and Sanford was the site of a naval air base during the war and for decades afterward.

As an adult, after I went through Imago Relationship Therapy with Susan, I sat down with my mother and father and discussed with them my early years. While I might not have been consciously aware of these circumstances, unconsciously I was very aware. Time of birth and birth order are important pieces of information to understand who we are.?

Shortly after my birth, my dad went to Europe to fight in the war. As an infant, I would look up into my mother's face and see someone who was terrified that she might not see her husband again. Later, for a short while at the end of the war, when my dad returned, I would have nothing to do with him. I didn't know who he was. It was a tough time in America. Younger generations have no idea of what my parents' generation went through and the sacrifices they made. My parents were born in the middle of the First World War, and as teenagers they suffered through the Great Depression of the 1930s with the rest of the country. At that time the nation was experiencing major unemployment, shortages of food, and homelessness. Few had any hope we would come out of it.

Then our country heard the nightmare stories from Europe of Hitler's war machine, followed by Japan's attack on Pearl Harbor. With America declaring war on Japan and then Germany, that generation entered a new phase of their stress-filled lives dealing with the rationing of food, cars, gasoline, and even tires. One positive of that terrible war is that it brought us out of the Great Depression. I was born in the middle of that time.

So why was I hysterical about my mother leaving me? Up to that time, I had never been away from her. During the war, we went from relative to relative as housing was short and we needed the assistance of our families. Then, one morning she was leaving me. Where did she go? She was going to the hospital to have my brother. For the first time I was experiencing separation anxiety.

Two years later I had to go to the hospital for some minor surgery. I recall my parents driving to the front of the hospital—and I was terrified. At less than five, I shouldn't know what a hospital is. In the back seat I remember going from one side of the car to the other as my parents were trying to get me to leave the car and go with them into this horrible place. Through much of my life I would have anxiety attacks when I went to doctors or was around hospitals.

Pastor Mulvaney from Calvary Assembly and I were strolling through the aisles of a local hospital in Orlando in 1978, discussing dealing with hospital visitation. He looked at me and asked, "John, is anything

# LIPOSUCTION OF YOUR SOUL—YOUR MIND, EMOTIONS, AND WILL

the matter? Your face is white as snow." I said, "I don't know." Feeling clammy and dizzy, I had to sit down on a chair in the hallway. I was feeling anxious just being in that hospital setting. I recall a number of times passing out in a doctor's office. Once as I was being treated for water on the knee, while a nurse was shaving part of my leg, I passed out.

Our childhood influences our lives in many ways—both negative and positive. Sometimes, our unconscious mind has unfinished business from childhood. I learned that that was so in my case. My separation anxiety at such a young age meant to me that Mommy was going to a bad place when she went to the hospital. Because of that experience, for much of my adult life I associated anything related to medicine as being bad.

Couples coming into my office often don't understand how childhood issues can affect us as adults. The childhood story I shared affected me through an entire lifetime. Whether or not we have a good childhood, our parents and caretakers can dramatically affect us in positive and negative ways. And as parents we can have the same dramatic effect on our own children. This chapter on strongholds of the mind, emotions, and will concerns is what I learned about certain journeys we all take through life and how we are affected by those journeys, even if we have a good childhood.

## Observation about Marriage

Harville Hendrix makes this observation about marriage: "In our society marriage is viewed as choose a mate, climb into a box, settle in and then take your first close look at who you married, stay put if you like what you see. If you don't like what you see, climb out of the box and scout around for another mate. Whether or not marriage works depends upon your ability to attract a good partner. The common solution to an unhappy marriage is to divorce and start over. Some couples stay in the box, tighten the lid, and put up with a disappointing relationship for the rest of their lives."[1]

Hendrix proposes a more hopeful view of love relationships. "Marriage is not some static state between two unchanging people; but rather it is a psychological and spiritual journey that, as romantic love began to play a more substantial role in mate selection, begins in the ecstasy of attraction, meanders through the rocky stretch of self-discovery, and ends in the creation of an intimate and joyful lifelong union. Whether you realize the full potential of this vision depends not on your ability to attract the perfect mate, but on your willingness to acquire knowledge about hidden parts of yourself." I would add to this a willingness to acquire knowledge about God's desire for you and your marriage.

## Journeys of Life

It would seem that we all have three pathways we take through life. Ironically, they all seem to be related to the development of romantic love. Hendrix calls these three pathways, life journeys. His names for these life journeys are the cosmic journey, the evolutionary journey, and the psychological journey.[2] While I have borrowed from that idea, I have merged the concept into my own understanding of God's impact on our lives. If, while learning more about ourselves, we become more aware of how our pathways were developed, we will be better equipped to connect with our partner in marriage.

### SPIRITUAL PATHWAY

Our internal mandate in this pathway is to be connected to God and to others. As we go through developmental stages, we have an inner desire for connection. When that connection is not there, we feel empty. We may be able to be on our own for a while, but then the desire for fellowship of some kind enters our thoughts.

This spiritual pathway begins the moment we are conceived. While in our mother's womb, we are connected to her by floating in an oceanic joy of euphoria. All of our needs were met, and we floated in comfort without any rejection. Some of us may experience at some deep level of our psyche the emotional experiences of our mother. If our mother went through extreme stress or depression, there seems to be evidence that we are affected even in our mother's womb. Not everyone is affected in that way, for we are protected in the womb in ways we will not experience for many years.

# LIPOSUCTION OF YOUR SOUL—YOUR MIND, EMOTIONS, AND WILL

But when we are born, our umbilical cord is torn from us, and we begin a lifetime of feeling rejected and wounded—as well as love—from our significant caretakers. Some wounds and rejection are serious, and some are not. The point is that we all shared an original connectedness with our mothers, and after that our entire lifetime is a mandate to reconnect to that original wholeness again, to return to our original state of being. We want to return to that inner sense of energy where we are joyful and satisfied.

Our real mandate of this spiritual pathway is to be connected with the Father for eternity. When that day comes, we will be truly connected with all of his creation, and our search will be over. Until that day comes, we can learn how to be connected with God through prayer, praise, and worship. Praise is what we do when we enter the gates of thanksgiving; worship is what we do when we arrive. True worship of our Father requires a real connection by going into his very presence, into the inner temple which is the Holy of Holies, the place where the Redeemer dwells. When we connect with God and experience his presence, and when we become the persons he wants us to be, we enter a deeper level of our lives. I believe the depth of our connection with God will determine our emotional health as well as our relational health with our spouse.

I challenge you now to enter into the Holy of Holies with your heavenly Father. You can repent for not being the husband or wife, mother or father, or man or woman he wants you to be. We can petition God through prayer to begin revealing to us how to become a godly person, and we can commit to journey with the Father and let him show us that we can become that person—no matter what painful experience we are having in life. We should not be moved by what we feel, or see, or think, but we should be moved only by the Word of God as it becomes present in our lives.

Because of our desire to be connected, God decided to give us "covenant marriage" while we are on this earth. God recognized it was not good for Adam to be alone, so he gave him Eve. Covenant marriage is a relationship based on a covenant with each other and with God where we learn how to love unconditionally, meet our partner's emotional and physical needs, and grow into spiritual maturity. When each marriage partner becomes truly committed to heal each other, then the dysfunctional family of origin cycle will be stopped and we can raise healed children. It is all about connection, and connection is the spiritual pathway to healing.

We have the opportunity to choose the blessings or the curses. We can stay under that cycle of dysfunction that generations tend to reproduce, or we can decide to live under the blessings—and change history.

## Our Environmental Pathway

Our internal mandate in the environmental pathway is to survive, to stay alive. We operate under an unconscious agenda that puts us in either a fight or flight mode when we undergo an unsafe life or relational experience. Harville Hendrix makes the analogy of animals in the forest. When they sense danger, they fight, flee, freeze, or cower.[3] When the animals are safe they mate, nurture what they mate, eat, sleep, work, and play.

If we feel emotionally unsafe in our committed relationships, we go into fight or flight survival modes of survival. I have worked with individuals in a relationship who went into freeze mode, like the chameleon lizard. I think of one wife in a physically abusive relationship who, when her husband came home, would try to blend into her environment and not be seen. We are merely going into a survival mode when we react like that. If we feel emotionally safe in our marriage, on the other hand, we experience an environment that allows us to be creative and passionate.

In his book *Man and his Animal Brain,*[4] neuroscientist Paul McLean looks at the three layers of our brain and how they work. One layer is the brain stem, which is our source of physical action. The brain stem controls vital physical systems from reproduction and sleep to blood circulation and muscle response. A second layer of the brain is the limbic system. This is the center of our intense feelings: sadness, joy, fear, anger, anxiety, and aggression. These first two layers are the source of automatic reactions. The limbic system is a pathway that links the brain stem and the third layer, the cerebral cortex. The cerebral cortex lies at the center of our cognitive functions. It is the part of the brain that helps us make decisions, think, observe, plan, anticipate, respond, and create ideas. It is the logical part of the brain, taking in data from the external world through our five senses. This data flows through neurological pathways through the amygdale in the limbic system, and a determination is developed in an instant whether our situation is safe or dangerous.

Many psychologists think that what we know as the unconscious mind is housed in the brain's limbic system, the center of our feelings. The unconscious mind has no awareness of time or its environment. Instead, it appears to register feelings. When we experience an event that is frustrating or hurtful, that data is sent to the limbic system. With an unconscious "knee jerk" response, our behavior shifts into fight or flight mode. We begin learning these behaviors as we develop from childhood, and until healing happens, we usually take them into our adult love relationships.

Our unconscious mind has only one mandate: to survive. So when we react to our partner in a hurtful experience, at an unconscious level we are trying to survive. Of course, we do not walk around saying, "This is my unconscious agenda reacting, so I am going to scream, throw something, slam a door, or leave." It is called the unconscious mind because we do not experience an awareness of our decisions. Remember, we are spirit, soul, and body. The will, emotions, and mind together make up the soul. The reason the generational curse (or family of origin issue) is so important to break and change the cycle is because it affects our very soul, comprised of our will, emotions, and mind.

## Our Connection Pathway

The people who most influence our lives are our parents or caretakers. A caretaker is an individual who gives physical or emotional care and support and who was involved in our development. Sometimes a caretaker influences us negatively more than positively. According to Harville Hendrix, the connection pathway consists of a socialization part of the process (where we learn how to deal with the outside world) and a nurturing part (where there was either warmth and availability or coldness and unavailability on the part of our caretakers.) How drastically the negative experiences affect us depends on various factors such as the historical timing of our birth, our birth order with our siblings, and the genetic disposition we are born with. Some individuals seem to react strongly to negative stimulus, while others do not.

## How Were You Nurtured?

During this nurturing part of our journey in childhood, we develop defensive adaptations when we are hurt, angry, scared, or frustrated. These behaviors gradually develop into how we deal with feeling unsafe in our adult love relationships. If our caretakers were over-involved in our upbringing by being intrusive, insensitive, invasive, controlling, or invalidating, we tend to be minimizers in adult love relationships. That is, we tend to withdraw, shut down, detach, or avoid attention. If our caretakers were under-involved in our upbringing by being avoidant, neglectful, unavailable, withdrawn, or uninterested, then we tend to develop into maximizers in adult love relationships. When feeling unsafe with our partner, we tend to cry, pursue, whine, cling, or attract attention.

This is where the power of the generational curse, or family of origin issues, sets in. We were raised by untutored parents, who were themselves raised by untutored parents, and so on. Because we are not really prepared for parenting (except as by our models growing up), we will make many mistakes and be totally unaware of our child's emotional needs in certain developmental stages. As they develop we will too often err by giving them far more information rather than affirmation.

Hendrix looked at what he calls "the birth of the social self."[5] He proposes four basic areas in which we are socialized: thinking, feeling (the polar opposite of thinking), acting, and sensing. Our caretakers may have influenced our thinking around these four basic areas. For example, they might have taught us that it is okay to think and solve problems. Or, it is okay to feel and to express your feelings, to take action, to be spontaneous or humorous, and to experience all one's body senses. Or our caregivers may have sent big-picture messages like it is okay to be you and it is okay to be.

Scripture says we are to bring up children according to their gifts: "Start children off on the way they should go, and even when they are old they will not turn from it" (Prov. 22:6 NIV). But many parents raise children according to what they want. Of course we are to guide our children as they mature, but how many parents push their children into career paths that are unsuitable for them? To be healthy adults raising healthy children, we have to send the message that it is okay to be.

# LIPOSUCTION OF YOUR SOUL—YOUR MIND, EMOTIONS, AND WILL

As individuals growing up we experienced caretakers who knew little of our developmental needs, and in many cases failed at meeting them. If we experienced either a lack of nurturing or a smothering experience, we will most likely take that into our adult love relationships, and ultimately into our marriage. That is, of course, unless those negative experiences were compensated for in our development. Because our caretakers were unaware of these needs, they would not have known to compensate for them. So this unfinished business becomes a part of our unconscious mind, with an unconscious agenda during adulthood.

The following Bible verses give scriptural evidence of the development we go through as individuals. If we received godly parenting, we stand an excellent chance of growing up with a sense of secure attachment. But if we were insecurely attached as children, we will feel insecurely attached in our marriage relationships.

- Deuteronomy 6:6–7: And these words which I command you today shall be in your heart, You shall teach them diligently to your children, and shall talk of them when you sit in your house, when you walk by the way, when you lie down, and when you rise up (NKJV).
- Psalm 103:13: As a father has compassion on his children, so the Lord has compassion on those who fear him (NIV).
- Psalm 119:9: How can a young man keep his way pure? By living according to your word (NIV).
- Proverbs 22:6: Train up a child in the way he should go and when he is old he will not depart from it (NKJV).
- Isaiah 49:15: Can a woman forget her nursing child, and not have compassion on the son of her womb? Surely they may forget, Yet I will not forget you (NKJV).
- 1 Thessalonians 2:7–8: We proved to be gentle among you, as a nursing mother tenderly cares for her own children. Having thus a fond affection for you, we were well-pleased to impart to you not only the gospel of God, but also our own lives, because you had become very dear to us (NASB).

If we did not experience good nurturing in our own development, it is not too late to change the cycle in the way we nurture our children, or even our grandchildren. It is also never too late to become healed as we learn about ourselves, learn relationship skills, and enter a deeper level with God and our spouse through connection.

## Exercise

## Who Is My Perfect Partner? (An Imago Relationship Therapy Exercise)

Read the sentences below and think of traits to fill in after the sentence.

1. Think of your childhood caretakers, and list up to five of their more dominant negative qualities, such as being absent, angry, busy, unavailable, depressed, controlling, and so on.

2. Think of frustrating times you had with your childhood caretakers, and list up to five of the more dominant feelings you recall. For example, did you feel abandoned, anxious, depressed, afraid, hopeless, ashamed, or inadequate? Did you have other feelings?

3. List up to five of their positive qualities of your childhood caretakers. For example, were they available, creative, faithful, supportive, hardworking, respectful, or did they have other similar qualities?

4. Think of the pleasant times you had with your childhood caretakers, and list up to five of the feelings you had about that. For example, did you feel loving, secure, excited, peaceful, happy, or playful?

5. List up to five ways you reacted as a child or teen to frustrating times. Did you, for example, talk to your friends about it,

# LIPOSUCTION OF YOUR SOUL—YOUR MIND, EMOTIONS, AND WILL

complain, become a super-achiever, isolate yourself, withdraw, use drugs, argue, drink, or criticize? What other behaviors come to mind?

Now take those characteristics and complete the following five sentences. After transferring the information, read it out loud to yourself to see what your relationship looks like. This is an exercise to see if the type of person you have been attracted to has some of the traits of your caretakers or past relationships.

1. I am trying to find or get a life partner who is (transfer traits from #3 above):

2. I want to begin to feel (transfer feelings from #4 above):

3. But I won't really fall in love unless some of these traits also are present (transfer traits from #1):

4. I often feel (transfer feelings from #2):

5. I have sometimes sabotaged getting my needs met because I (transfer responses from #5):

Now ask yourself, "Does my present relationship sound similar to some of this? If it does, those childhood experiences or past relationships in some ways describe our relationship with our "perfect partner." For most couples in a romantic relationship, there are usually similarities. Understanding why this happens is one of the goals of Imago Relationship Therapy.

*Chapter Five*
---

# IF YOU WANT TO BE RIGHT, YOU'RE GOING TO BE LONELY!

> You can learn a lot more from listening than you can from talking. Find someone with whom you don't agree in the slightest and ask them to explain themselves at length. Then take a seat, shut your mouth, and don't argue back. It's physically impossible to listen with your mouth open.
> —John Moe (radio host and author of *Conservative Me*)

ANGER POURED OUT of their mouths as a middle-aged couple in my office shouted at and interrupted each other. There was no way either was listening to or understanding the other. Finally, Cathy imploded in tears while Ted sat in stone-faced silence, looking at the tears of pain streaming down her face.

This type of pain between two individuals in a romantic relationship occurs all too often in our culture. I stopped this debate by asking each one what they were trying to protect—what were they defending. Ted and Cathy were both trying to be right in this argument, and that is what they were defending—the need to be right! They had already been to several sessions in my office, and I was beginning to teach them a skill so their conversations could stay in an adult-to-adult mode. Yet they still struggled to understand each other.

Needing to be right in a love relationship will leave us feeling disconnected, alone, and in conflict. Needing to be right is actually a defensive move so we can feel better about ourselves. (Paradoxically, we never do.) When we get triggered by our partner and react by a fight or flight action, we are defending a position. Usually, however, we are not aware that we are being defensive. We just feel like our partner needs to agree with, or at least understand, our position. Defending is almost always a reactionary behavior. We need to ask ourselves what we do when we are defending, and alternatively what we do when we are in a learning mode. If we can answer that, we can be more self-aware of our position in a conflict with our partner.

There have been times where Susan and I would be in a conflict, and we would both try proving that our position was the only one. Clueless as to what was really going on between us, we would exhaust ourselves trying to prove our points. Later, in marriage therapy, we learned the concept of "defend and learn." When I asked myself what I did when I was in "defend" mode and what I did when I was in "learn" mode, I saw that when I was defensive I would be cynical and closed, and not listening to what Susan was saying.

The specific content is not the issue. What is at issue is misunderstanding and not listening to each other. Hearing only what I thought Susan was saying, I would then react from my own defensive position by being cynical. I don't know why I couldn't see it wasn't working. Somehow we can't see the futility of our defensive reactions. We just keep on doing them, getting nowhere, and arguing perpetually.

I also looked at what I did when I was in "learn" mode, which is a position of trying to understand what my wife was trying to say in the conflict. At these times I was open, listening, and more attentive to her needs. I would be looking through her eyes to try to understand her position.

But in our conflicts I rarely stayed in "learn" and primarily got into "defend." For some couples, the argument goes on for years—without ever resolving the conflict. One would think we would wake up. Instead, we sink deeper into hopelessness and despair. The longer that dynamic exists, the worse the relationship. We interrupt each other, talk over each other, and often raise our voices to try convincing our partner that we are right and they are wrong. We become more convinced that our partner is crazy and wants only to hurt us, disagree with us, and humiliate us. We sink even deeper into hopelessness until the only way out is to leave

# IF YOU WANT TO BE RIGHT, YOU'RE GOING TO BE LONELY!

each other and divorce. This "communication" style is what we in the Imago Therapy community call "shoot reload communication."

## You Don't Have to Attend Every Argument You are Invited to!

When couples get to the shoot and reload point, it is difficult to restore the hope that they can actually fall in love again. This is a sad commentary on relationships.

At a conference a few years ago, I heard author John Bradshaw say he believes that the basis for all human issues and struggles is shame. If so, then the need to be right is our way to mask our fear of failure, fear of rejection, fear of incompetence, fear of engulfment, fear of separateness, and many other fears we develop out of shame. These are messages born in our childhood that come from those who most influenced us: our caretakers. Were those messages based on shame or based on affirmation and encouragement?

Applying the biblical concept of leaving our mothers and fathers and cleaving to our spouse means we have to separate our emotional self from our family of origin issues. This is difficult through a cognitive therapy approach to counseling that attempts to help counselees overcome difficulties by identifying and changing dysfunctional behaviors and thought processes. A therapeutic process of going through the feeling and grieving work helps us leave our family of origin emotionally. That does not mean we never see them again. It means we separate ourselves from any pain or hurt we incurred during our childhood and leave it in the past. It also means we develop healthy boundaries to separate ourselves from any intrusive behavior from family members trying to influence our marriage.

## A Cherokee Story Goes Like This

One evening an old Cherokee told his grandson about a battle that goes on inside people. "My son, the battle is between two wolves inside us all," he said. "One is evil. It is anger, envy, jealousy, sorrow, regret, greed, arrogance, self-pity, guilt, resentment, inferiority, lies, false pride, superiority, and ego. The other is good. It is joy, peace, love, hope, serenity, humility, kindness, benevolence, empathy, generosity, truth, compassion, and faith."

The grandson thought about it for a minute. Then he asked his grandfather, "Which wolf wins?"

The old Cherokee simply replied, "The one you feed."

This points back to the biblical concept of renewing the mind. We can choose to learn to truly understand our partner and move to an empathic understanding of what they are feeling. To do this, we need to feed our good wolf.

## How Shame Affects Our Love Life

One of the earliest books on shame was written by the Renaissance genius Annibale Pocaterra. It was called *Due Dialogi Della Vergogna (Two Dialogues on Shame)*. Pocaterra wrote, "There is an innate and a learned component to emotion . . . there must be two shames, one natural and free from awareness and the other acquired, moved by reason, and led by understanding." (For more information see Donald Nathanson's *Shame and Pride* published by W.W. Norton & Co.) This author wrote hundreds of years ago about good shame (discretion, humility, and reverence) and bad shame (disgrace or humiliation), which author John Bradshaw further looks at in his book *Healing The Shame That Binds You*.[1]

Bradshaw writes that "Healthy shame is an emotion that teaches us about our limits and like all emotions, moves us to get our basic needs met." In other words, healthy shame covers or protects us when we need to be covered or protected. Healthy shame is an internal dialogue that creates humility and helps us appreciate our partner or spouse. He further states, "Unhealthy shame, which is humiliation, exposes us when we need to be covered." A person can believe with unhealthy shame that his or her whole self is fundamentally flawed and defective. From unhealthy shame an individual develops self-hatred and self-loathing. This idea of shame is so important because it goes to how we are projecting ourselves onto our partner.

Relationship projection is like watching the old Super 8 mm family movies. We see the image on a screen, but the source of that image is at the projector when light passes through the film to project the image on a screen. In relationships, we often project what we hate about ourselves onto our partner. We see our partner as flawed, when at times the flaw is in ourselves.

Bradshaw further states that there is a good shame and a bad shame, like good cholesterol and bad cholesterol. Good shame is discretion or humility. It is feeling little and diminished in the presence of mystery. Good shame is also feeling speechless in relation to the immensity of what one is experiencing; we feel an urge to kneel or hide our face and eyes. We may be rapt in awe and filled with fear, but we are fascinated. We know it is okay to be vulnerable and to make mistakes, to need and ask for help, to feel confused and want to learn, and to know that there is something greater than ourselves.

This is our experience when we begin the journey of repentance. When we enter the presence of God in the Holy of Holies, this is exactly what we experience. Aristotle said, "Lovers look into each other's eyes, not at the other parts of their bodies. For in the eyes *Aidas* (shame) dwells." Bad shame, however, is disgrace or humiliation. When this occurs, an individual feels exposed, little, flawed, defective, shy, embarrassed, or diminished. The individual experiences an attack on the self—by the self—through self-blame, self-contempt, self-loathing, or self-hatred. That individual feels powerless with no place to hide. He or she is sometimes speechless or paralyzed. I have seen many husbands speechless, as if they are afraid of saying the wrong thing. They are like turtles sticking their heads out of the shell, only to have a hail storm come.

When bad shame rules our life, we develop defending scripts to cover up the shame or self-hatred we feel. John Bradshaw writes that some of these scripts use perfection to cover up the feeling of failure, blame to cover up self-blame, acting righteous to cover up sinfulness, critical contempt to cover up self-contempt, and rage to cover up feeling incompetent. Silvan Tomkins states that "Shame strikes at the heart of man . . . shame is felt as an inner torment, a thickness of the soul . . . defeated, alienated, lacking in dignity, or worth." Tompkins writes of nine innate affects, which are primarily displayed in facial behavior. They are what our partner sees when we are in a positive or a negative frame.

Bradshaw states that the primary blueprint leading to our decision-making is provided by what is called the Affect System. The Affect System is composed of the parts of the nervous system that process positive and negative information in order to execute appropriate actions. Without feeling, however, nothing matters—and with it anything can matter. When we are in a positive mindset, our affect or feeling system will project that. Likewise, when we are in a negative mindset, our facial behavior will project that, too. This helps explain why so many arguments develop out of what someone perceives their partner is feeling, and why that partner is so often unaware of projecting these emotions.

I remember the first time I became aware of this. Decades ago, when I was in the entertainment business, we videoed our stage show to see how we looked. I had been convinced I had a great smile and was really projecting. Then I saw the playback. There I stood with little expression on my face and only a semi-smile. We don't have much of an idea how our facial expressions look to others. Comedians spend years in front of a mirror practicing their facial expressions in order to see what others see when they do a routine. Look at Jim Carey and imagine the hours he must have spent in mirror time.

I realized another example of this from playing saxophone. People were always saying how loud I was, yet I didn't think I was that loud. After all, I could hardly hear myself. Then I realized the sound of a saxophone goes forward—and I was behind that projection. I was unable to experience what others were hearing. The same is true of conflict in relationships. Often we are not aware of what our partner is seeing. Our partner keeps saying that we are yelling, or that we look so mad, and we keep feeling they are hallucinating. Unless we walk around with a mirror and a monitor for our voice, we have very little idea what our partner is experiencing. It might be interesting to keep a mirror handy so we could put it in front of ourselves in a conflict.

In the middle 1800s the Hassidic rabbi known as Menahem Mendel of Kotz made a most profound statement:

> If I am I because I am I
> And you are you because you are you
> Then I am and you are.
> But if I am I because you are you and
> You are you because I am I
> Then I am not and you are not.

# IF YOU WANT TO BE RIGHT, YOU'RE GOING TO BE LONELY!

This is certainly an early comment on co-dependency. In other words, there needs to be an "I" for there to be a "we." Most individuals focus on the "we" instead of the "I." It is critical in relationships to move forward to a status of differentiation—which means that I am connected to this person, and I am okay with that. But we have our individuality, and I am okay with that, too. We fear neither separation nor engulfment. The fear of separation occurs when we long for our partner to be like us. But our partner is an individual, so that person cannot be identical to us—or to anyone else. The fear of engulfment comes when we fear being swallowed by the relationship, thus losing ourselves. It does not have to be that way.

I have called this chapter, "If You Want to Be Right, You're Going to be Lonely." This refers to more than just being bull-headed. It often comes from unfinished business from our past, which sets up a knee-jerk reaction. The defensive mechanism that causes us to need to be right in a conflict with our partner is a sad commentary on our own arrogance. There are times in my counseling when, listening to couples, it sounds like they live on different planets—and sometimes different universes. John Gray may have it right when he wrote *Men Are From Mars, Women Are From Venus*. Each individual is totally convinced that they heard what they thought they heard and said what they thought they said. That means they know they are right and their partner is wrong.

Most couples who come to my office say they have communication problems. That usually ends up with them blaming each other instead of trying to understand each other. But usually it is not a communication problem. Rather, it is a connection problem. Many people think that bad communication leads to disconnection. In reality, disconnection leads to bad communication. Problems in a relationship are not caused by differences, but by how the couple handles those differences. At the root of the problem is the fear that our partner is different from us.

In her recent book, *How To Improve Your Marriage Without Talking About It*,[2] Pat Love shares a very interesting concept. In her research, she has looked for the reason women need to talk with their husbands—and why most men would rather get some distance from that idea. The two words men fear most from their wives are, "Let's talk." It seems that men take "let's talk" as implying they have done something wrong, triggering their shame of failing as protectors and providers. On the other hand, it seems that when women are not able to talk and connect with their partners, they experience a basic fear of isolation and deprivation. Couples need to learn to interact through healthy approaches that create some level of emotional safety. As I said earlier, conflict is growth trying to happen.

## The Couple's Dialogue

I have previously mentioned that most couples in a conflict use a type of communication style Imago therapists call "shoot reload communication." That is what Ted and Cathy were doing, which I described at the beginning of this chapter. This occurs when one person fires a verbal frustration at their partner, and the other person is primarily thinking about what they want to say in response, and then firing back. Very little listening happens. The other partner responds by doing the same thing. Back and forth this interaction goes. It is like a perpetual argument with no end and no resolve. For some couples, it goes on for years. Neither partner truly understands the other because neither is truly listening or trying to understand what the other is saying.

No wonder many men are so reluctant to talk to women who say they need to discuss their issues. James 1:19 says, "This you know, my beloved brethren, but everyone must be quick to hear, slow to speak and slow to anger" (NASB). Instead, if we are slow to listen and quick to speak, we will be quick to wrath. Though written long ago and far away, the Bible is truly a great psychology book.

Conflict does not come because of our differences; it comes because at a deep level we feel misunderstood. Conflict exists only when one or both partners feel misunderstood. We all long for someone to truly understand us. If that is the case, we have to ask ourselves my favorite question from Dr. Phil: "How is that working for you?" Obviously it is not. Yet we continue to use this method, somehow hoping we will finally get our point across and win the argument. It has been my experience that often couples really want the same thing. But because they are not really listening to each other, they fail to really understand each other.

# IF YOU WANT TO BE RIGHT, YOU'RE GOING TO BE LONELY!

We need to have a way to see our partner's world as it appears to our partner, not just as it looks to us. Since we usually see our partner's world only through our own perspective, it is no wonder so many couples sink deeper into a power struggle.

As I wrote earlier in this chapter, communication comes in only two packages: to protect and defend (closed), or to understand and learn (open). I often ask couples what they do when they are in defending and what they do when they are in learning. One can get to resolution in a difference with one's partner only from the open position, the "learning" mode.

Bruce Wood, an Imago Therapy colleague, wrote about "polarization," which happens when partners become angry with one another. A small misunderstanding grows into a huge argument.

Wood writes that polarization involves a sequence of beliefs:

1. I feel misunderstood by my partner.
2. My needs are not being met by my partner.
3. My partner doesn't want to meet my needs (or he/she doesn't care about me).
4. My partner is hostile and malicious.
5. I can't be me and be loved by my partner, who doesn't see or hear me and doesn't want to.
6. Whatever I do for my partner isn't appreciated or isn't enough.
7. Why be in this relationship at all?

Both partners progress down a similar track, entertaining the same sequence of beliefs and becoming more and more distant. This sequence gets triggered by partners when they are overwhelmed by fears and frustrations.

When Harville Hendrix and Helen Hunt began developing Imago Relationship Therapy, they created the foundation piece to build the rest of the model. It came to be known as the "Couple's Dialogue." It has also been referred to as the "Intentional Dialogue," meaning "I intend to stay in this dialogue until we both understand each other, not to decide who is right and who is wrong, but simply to understand each other."

## Mirroring

The first part of the dialogue, called *mirroring,* is repeating the words back that you have heard your partner say. This does not mean you merely parrot your partner's words, because that would lack genuineness. Instead, to mirror your partner means repeating what they said with a genuine effort to make sure you heard what they actually said, and to understand them. As many couples have learned, this is not an easy skill, especially for those who may be used to going into the shoot reload style of communication. It is very difficult to shut down our defensive posture when trying to exercise this listening skill. That is why we eventually have to learn to go to our partner's island to see through their eyes what is being experienced. It can be amazing when we actually learn we are living with another person besides ourselves. When we mirror our partner, that doesn't mean we have to agree with them. It means we merely reflect their information to be sure we heard what they said and to know we can respond when they are finished.

## Validation

The goal of mirroring is to move to what Hendrix calls *validation.* Validation does not necessarily mean having to agree with our partner. It means respecting our partner's right to have a viewpoint that might differ from ours. Validation means making sense of what our partner is sharing by looking at the issue through their eyes. Hedy Schleifer, an Imago Relationship colleague, uses the concept of an island. Imagine you and your partner are on two islands in the ocean. On your individual islands, you have a reality that is based on all of the messages you have received in your life—both positive and negative.

The problem is that in a conflict, partners tend to stay on their own islands. But we can develop an imaginary bridge—called *dialogue*—between our two islands. Using the Couple's Dialogue, we go to each other's island to try to understand what the other person is saying. When I use this metaphor with couples, it helps them go to each other's island and understand what their position is based on. I usually have couples facing each other and looking into each other's eyes. I want them to be thinking, "Let that person show up as he or she really is, and not as

# IF YOU WANT TO BE RIGHT, YOU'RE GOING TO BE LONELY!

whom I think he or she is. We often hear the statement, "You don't know what it is like until you walk in my shoes." That is true, and dialogue is a way to do that with our partners.

Hendrix feels that we are in a symbiotic relationship in the power struggle. This means that as long as my partner thinks like I think, talks like I talk, and makes the same decisions I make, then my partner is right. If they do anything else, they are wrong—because my right is the only right. Admitting this to ourselves can be difficult. But after all, that is why we are in a power struggle. It is because of our need to be right.

There is a concept in Imago Relationship Therapy called the *other*. If I am in a symbiotic relationship, there is no other, there is only me, my way. Until Susan became the other, there was no relationship. There has to be an other for there to be a relationship.

Going deeper with this idea, until there is an other, love does not exist. For me to be in love with my wife, she has to be the other. Many couples think they are in love, but this cannot be true unless there is an other. If we don't allow our partner to be the other, we really are just in love with ourselves. We are only fooling ourselves. In actuality, we are self-centered and self-focused. We are programmed to be that way, and the church has not changed that. Selfishness is just as rampant in the church as in secular society, and we need to get rid of our spiritual pride, humble ourselves, and let God be God—with us as his children.

When we validate our partner, we allow them to become our *other*.

## Empathy

The goal of *validation* is to move to *empathy*, which is the bond that brings a couple to connection. Empathy is understanding what our partner feels when we have hurt, angered, or scared them. We all long for someone to understand our deepest feelings and hurts. When our partner does not, we feel hopeless and helpless. But when our partner truly understands what we are feeling during conflicts, we feel a weight being lifted, and we feel connected. Empathy should be our goal in the couple's dialogue.

A man was riding the subway in New York. At one of the stops, he noticed two children get on, along with what appeared to be their father. As he noticed the body language in all three, he knew these kids were going to cause problems. The children began running all over the subway car playing, with no regard for others. The man sat down and just looked out the window, staring into space. The children were throwing things, sometimes hitting older people with what they threw. The man just sat there, not doing anything about his children. Finally, an observer could not take it anymore. He went over to their father and said, "Excuse me, but are you aware your children are causing problems for others on this car?" The man looked up, startled, and said, "No! I'm sorry. I just left the hospital. My wife died three hours ago." Immediately, the observer saw this father as a grieving widower, whereas a moment ago he saw him as a terrible father. This is empathy.

I remember when I got this "Aha! Moment" with my wife during one of our couple's dialogues. I suddenly saw her as not a nagging wife, but as a wife who felt invisible and unimportant. A moment before this revelation I felt I could do no right for her, but now I was able to completely reframe how I looked at her. When I reframed her through empathy, I also saw that the reason I felt I was being criticized was that I was projecting onto her my own issues. As I wrote earlier, in relationship projection, we often see in our partner what is really inside us. But because we don't want to admit that, we feel we need always to be right.

So this dialogue has as its parts: *mirroring, validation,* and *empathy.* Barbara J. Reichlin, an Imago Relationship Therapy colleague in Bellaire, Texas, uses a wonderful approach to build intimacy through this dialogue. (Her website is *www.imagoworks.com.*) She calls it "Build Intimacy and Great Communication Skills in Just 20 Days." With her permission I have borrowed some of her ideas below. Try using this over the next week to build intimacy and communication skills with your partner. Use one of these ideas each day, using the ideas of mirroring, validation, and empathy.

> Day one—Something I appreciate about you is:
> Day two—Something I like about us as a couple is:
> Day three—Something you do that helps me feel close to you is:
> Day four—A special memory of our relationship is the time when:
> Day five—Three things I find very romantic are:
> Day six—If I could change anything about myself, one thing I would change would be:

# IF YOU WANT TO BE RIGHT, YOU'RE GOING TO BE LONELY!

Day seven—Romance to me is:
And a way I think we could become more romantic is:

In my office recently a wife told her husband, "You don't know me." He said, "Of course I know you." She countered back, "No, you don't know me." It took him a while to connect the dots and realize there is a difference between knowing and *knowing*. One way of knowing is to *know things about her*. But she was talking about *knowing her heart*, which is a much deeper level. Many of us know *about* God, but do we *know* him? To really know God we need to spend time with him. To know our partner means we have to spend intimate time with them and truly understand their heart—not what we project onto them out of our own issues.

## Couples Exercise

Do you recall the beginning of your relationship, when you first fell in love? Describe your behavior at that time.

Describe your partner's behavior.

When we move out of the infatuation stage of love, we often stop doing the very behaviors that caused the chemistry between us. We stop doing things like gazing into our partner's eyes, flirting, being playful, and giving thoughtful love gifts.

What do you no longer do that you did when you were infatuated?

What has your partner stopped doing?

What behaviors would you like to restore to your relationship?

What things frustrate you that your partner does?

What could you do differently to create an environment for a more positive response from your partner?

*Chapter Six*

# SLAYING THE GIANT-KILLERS IN YOUR RELATIONSHIP

IS UNFORGIVENESS HINDERING your relationship with God? Or someone else? This is the burning question.

My office was thick with the hurt and pain of a couple who had come to me for help. Jennifer had imploded. She sobbed uncontrollably, with tears streaming down her cheeks. She had a look of hopelessness, mixed with pleading and gloom. Her mouth quivered as she cried out, trying to make sense of what had happened. A moment before, she had been yelling at her husband with contempt and rage, her fists clenched so tightly that her fingernails could have cut into her hand. Jennifer glared at her husband for what he had done to her. His first affair had cut into her heart, and these current emotions were coming from the discovery that her husband had a second affair years later.

Here they were, twelve months after the second affair came to light, with her anger and shame still at a high. In the past year of therapy the husband was doing everything he could to make up for the pain, including being totally accountable, coming to individual therapy, and participating in couple's therapy. He was trying to save his marriage and willing to do anything.

After a year of this, however, he was sitting in my office looking at the floor, his shoulders drooping with the weight of not knowing what to do, looking discouraged and hopeless. Although she had come with her husband to therapy, she would not go see a therapist individually to talk through her anger, nor would she try to come to grips with the pain she was feeling. Yet she would not leave him.

Jennifer had every right to her emotions. Unfortunately, she had moved into the "victim" stage of grieving, where the root of bitterness had set in. She was stuck in that stage and would not let go to move forward with her life. Whether or not she stayed with her husband, she needed forgiveness in her heart to put the bitterness behind her. In the "victim" stage, self-righteousness runs at an all-time high. This very hurt person was stuck. She could not leave, for fear of tearing her family apart. Yet in staying she was doing more damage to the whole family. This is how confusing life can be when we don't forgive. She had a giant in her life that was bigger than the affair. That giant was bitterness, and it stopped her from getting on with her life and either healing the marriage or ending it.

One giant that can radically stop a marriage from reaching its God-given potential is resentment, or the root of bitterness. That is a tough giant to slay, and if we allow it to take root in our lives toward one who hurt us, we invite chaos, psychological issues, and physiological issues. One way to create the environment for safety and passion in our relationship is to learn how to walk in forgiveness when someone—especially our partner—hurts us. Unresolved hurts, whether in childhood or adulthood, can lead to bitterness or unforgiveness.

## We Want Grace for Ourselves and Perfection for Everyone Else!

The topic of the previous chapter, on blaming others and having the need to always be right, naturally progresses to this chapter on the giant-killers of bitterness and unforgiveness. The couples I see often are so bitter and unforgiving that they find it almost impossible to get out of the rut in their relationship. And as we often hear, a rut is a grave with both ends knocked out. All couples need to know how failing to forgive leads to difficulty in receiving God's blessings.

No matter how deep the hurt, an individual who knows God can forgive more easily than one who does not. This is a point where the church is falling down on the job and failing to help marriages. With the teachings of repentance, blood covenant, and the marriage covenant so seldom being heard in the church, it is no wonder that many couples have difficulty with their commitment to marriage, not to mention their commitment to God. So many Christians want to walk in grace for their sins but expect perfection for everyone else who has hurt us or wronged us. I am glad God does not look at grace that way, for godly grace is unmerited favor from God.

## Faith Will Not Work in an Unforgiving Heart—in the Midst of Disharmony!

Do you ever wonder why your prayers or those of others you know rarely if ever seem to be answered? Look at what the Word tells us:

> But I urge you and entreat you, brethren, by the name of our Lord Jesus Christ, that all of you be in perfect harmony and full agreement in what you say, and that there be no dissensions or factions or divisions among you, but that you be perfectly united in your common understanding and in your opinions and judgments.
> —1 Cor. 1:10 AMPLIFIED

Faith will not work in an unforgiving heart. I have said it before and I will say it again: The Bible is the best psychology book ever written. So often in a selfish society we don't know how to live and work as a team. We always want to be right, and when that is the prevailing interest in a relationship struggle, both partners usually lose. In a dysfunctional relationship, one that is not in harmony, we cannot receive the blessings that are available when we are in harmony. There is just too much negative energy in force.

The word *emotion* really means *energy motion*. You might recall an argument between you and your partner. The more serious the disagreement, the more weight we feel on our shoulders. That weight is a negative energy that erodes faith. When that happens, it is difficult to pray in faith and believe the answer will come. Becoming a team must be a priority in all areas of marriage, including finances, parenting, careers, and goals.

> For as long as [there are] envying and jealousy and wrangling and factions among you, are you not unspiritual and of the flesh, behaving yourselves after a human standard and like mere (unchanged) men?
> —1 Cor. 3:2–3 AMPLIFIED

Look at what the apostle Paul writes in First Corinthians: "For we are fellow workmen (joint promoters, laborers together) with and for God; you are God's garden and vineyard and field under cultivation, [you are] God's building" (3:9 AMPLIFIED).

Remember that the Bible calls marriage the model of the bride and bridegroom. The Scriptures encourage us to be a team working together: "Let each man of you love his wife as his very own self; and let the wife see that she respects and reverences her husband" (Eph. 5:33 AMPLIFIED). We are to work for the common good and build not our kingdom but the kingdom of God. This doesn't mean we cannot have individuality in a relationship, but it does mean we should honor those differences as strengths and not let them cause conflicts. I realize that is so difficult in the power struggle that disconnects us with our partners.

When we honor each other in relationships and do not feel the need to control the relationship, more harmony and piece exists. And it becomes far easier to tap into the creative juices that are in all individuals to become successful at what God calls us to be. That is not the case, though, when we are in disharmony, for the negative energy blocks that from happening. Our society programs us to have negative energy, which is contrary to the Word of God. Remember, faith is energized action.

## There Must Be a Cleansing of Ourselves

> Now I rejoice, not that you were made sorry, but that your sorrow led to repentance. For you were made sorry in a godly manner, that you might suffer loss from us in nothing. For godly sorrow produces repentance leading to salvation, not to be regretted; but the sorrow of the world produces death. For observe this very thing, that you sorrowed in a godly manner: What diligence it produced in you, what clearing of yourselves, what indignation, what fear, what vehement desire, what zeal, what vindication! In all things you proved yourselves to be clear in this matter.
> —2 Cor. 7:9–11 NKJV

# SLAYING THE GIANT-KILLERS
# IN YOUR RELATIONSHIP

*Repentance* means "change of mind." The apostle Paul describes when a godly sorrow worked the right kind of repentance. As I wrote in the first chapter, the beauty of repentance is the cleansing of the individual as a spiritual experience in which we go into the presence of God. When we enter the inner temple to experience God's faithfulness and unconditional love through grace, we have to learn to leave pride and selfishness at the door.

In the temple in Jerusalem described in the Old Testament, there was an outer court and an inner court. The high priest was the only one allowed into the inner court to make atonement for the people of Israel. This is where the priest would enter the presence of God. In the book of Revelation we are told that Jesus "has made us kings and priests to His God and Father . . ." (1:6 NKJV). No longer do we have to wait for the priest to atone for us once a year. As priests we can now go into the presence of God through repentance.

As I have previously written, I experienced going into the presence of God through repentance firsthand during the separation my wife and I went through. This type of repentance is a journey, not a single event. Through it we receive a cleansing, and we form a new heart that others will notice. When a couple experiences this journey, the cleansing between them is like a Shekinah glory where the presence of God comes down on them. That kind of anointing can come only from our Father.

Repentance, however, does not eliminate the consequences of our actions. Many couples I meet struggle to understand this principle. When a man has been unfaithful, I commonly hear something like "That is in the past. Let's move forward." After he has been discovered, it is as if there are no consequences to that unfaithful act. Repentance cleanses us before God, and true repentance is not asking God on Sunday to forgive us for what we are going to do on Monday. A person who has been betrayed needs to see the pattern of the new person; the trust must be earned, not demanded.

In his book *Repentance*, Richard Owen Roberts writes on the "Seven Maxims of Repentance."[1] The seven maxims are as follows:

1. True repentance is a gift of God.
2. True repentance is not a single act, but an ongoing continual attitude.

3. True repentance is not merely turning from what you have done, but also from what you are.
4. True repentance is not what you do for yourself, but what you do for God.
5. True repentance is not turning away merely from the fruits of sin, but from the very roots. If one repents merely of the fruits of sin (the consequences of being caught), the roots of the sin will continue to bear fruit. It not just the behavior, but the core issue, the root problem which causes the behaviour. If the core issues are not dealt with, the old behavior will continue to resurface.
6. True repentance is not secret, but open. The consequences of our behavior have hurt someone: perhaps our spouse, our children, or someone else. So why would true repentance be done only in secret between an individual and God? Repairing the conflict means there has to be an outward manifestation of that proclamation.
7. True repentance is both negative and positive. It is not just turning from the sin, but also turning toward God through our relationship with him.

First John 1:9 assures us that "If we confess our sins, He is faithful and just to forgive us our sins and to cleanse us from all unrighteousness" (NKJV). What a glorious experience when a married couple in crisis can reach that place as a revelation to them. 1 John 2:9–11 states,

> Whoever says he is in the Light and hates his brother is in darkness even until now. Whoever loves his brother abides in the Light, and in It or in him there is no occasion for stumbling or cause for error or sin. But he who hates his brother is in darkness and walking in the dark; he is straying and does not perceive or know where he is going, because the darkness has blinded his eyes (AMPLIFIED).

We usually think the word "hate" means to detest. But the original Greek word used in this passage of Scripture, *miseo*, actually means "to love someone less than someone else." The ministry of God is all about reconciliation," but it is in our selfish culture to want what is best for us—not what is best for the marriage.

# SLAYING THE GIANT-KILLERS
# IN YOUR RELATIONSHIP

The book of Leviticus (19: 16–18) teaches us three ways we can hate our brother. First, we can hate audibly: "You shall not go up and down as a dispenser of gossip and scandal among your people, nor shall you endanger the life of your neighbor" (AMPLIFIED). Verse sixteen teaches us to not go about as a talebearer. Second, we can hate with our attitude: "You shall not hate your brother in your heart; but you shall surely rebuke your neighbor, lest you incur sin because of him" (AMPLIFIED). Verse seventeen tells us to not hate our brother in our hearts—in other words, to not judge them or form opinions about them. Third, we can hate through our actions: "You shall not take revenge or bear any grudge against the sons of your people, but you shall love your neighbor as yourself" (AMPLIFIED). Verse eighteen tells us to not take vengeance nor bear any grudge, but to love the neighbor as ourselves.

We need a strong conviction to stand on a belief and not cave in because of selfishness and blaming our partner. I understand the pain individuals go through in an unhealthy marriage. But the Bible tells us about having the goal of a healthy, godly marriage to keep us from ever getting to the pain of divorce. I have said before that couples don't want divorce; they want an end to pain. Second Timothy 2:20–21 reads, "But in a great house there are not only vessels of gold and silver, but also of wood and clay, some for honor and some for dishonor. Therefore if anyone cleanses himself from the latter, he will be a vessel for honor, sanctified and useful for the Master, prepared for every good work" (NKJV).

The power of repentance creates an ability to have a new heart or a new attitude. When we have a new heart, we will be a vessel for honor and prepared for every good work. When we feel connected with our partner, we feel safe and secure. But when we feel disconnected from our partner, we often feel like a boat adrift in the sea, so helpless and hopeless that we doubt we can ever feel safe again. Cleansing ourselves and taking ownership prepares us to have "every good work" in our marriage.

## The Consequences of Unforgiveness

The gospel of Matthew 18:18–20 has this: "Assuredly, I say to you, whatever you bind on earth will be bound in heaven, and whatever you loose on earth will be loosed in heaven. Again I say to you that if two of you agree on earth concerning anything that they ask, it will be done for them by My Father in heaven. For where two or three are gathered together in My name, I am there in the midst of them" (NKJV).

I have seen this truth in my own marriage. As Susan and I stood together in prayer, blessings have come forth in our own lives and those of our adult kids and grandkids. Harmony and agreement are powerful weapons against the negative energy and obstacles we face in our lives.

In Matthew 18:21–35, the parable of the unforgiving servant, Peter asks Jesus, "Lord, how often shall my brother sin against me, and I forgive him? Up to seven times?" (18:21 NKJV). The rest of this story presents a fascinating principle, which I call wanting "grace for ourselves and perfection for everyone else." A servant came before his king, asking for patience over his debts. The king was moved with compassion and forgave the debt. Then the servant went out and made his fellow servants pay their debts or be put in prison. When the king who had forgiven him heard of this, he delivered the servant to the torturers until he should pay all his debts. Verse thirty-five says, "So My heavenly Father also will do to you if each of you, from his heart, does not forgive his brother his trespasses" (NKJV).

## When you agree in prayer, Jesus is in your midst and prayer will work.

First Peter 3:7 states, "Husbands, likewise, dwell with them [wives] with understanding, giving honor to the wife, as to the weaker vessel, and as being heirs together of the grace of life, that your prayers may not be hindered" (NKJV).

This is the only key to answered prayers in marriage. If we are not honoring the individual with whom we entered into marriage covenant, no wonder our prayers go unanswered. Without honor, there is too much negative energy in the relationship. Peter also says, "Finally, all of you be of one mind, having compassion for one another; love as brothers, be tenderhearted, be courteous; not returning evil for evil or reviling for reviling, but on the contrary blessing, knowing that you were called to this, that you may inherit a blessing" (3:8-9 NKJV).

# SLAYING THE GIANT-KILLERS
# IN YOUR RELATIONSHIP

Peter is writing that we were called to inherit a blessing and not a curse. To do this we have to put the principle of intentionality into our journey with our spouse, and make a goal of reaching a relationship that truly is like heaven on earth.

## The Negative Power of Discord or Unforgiveness

> Who is wise and understanding among you? Let him show by good conduct that his works are done in the meekness of wisdom. But if you have bitter envy and self-seeking in your hearts, do not boast and lie against the truth. This wisdom does not descend from above, but is earthly, sensual, demonic. For where envy and self-seeking exist, confusion and every evil thing will be there. But the wisdom that is from above is first pure, then peaceable, gentle, willing to yield, full of mercy and good fruits, without partiality and without hypocrisy. Now the truth of righteousness is sown in peace by those who make peace.
>
> —James 3:13-18 NKJV

Years ago Derek Prince wrote a wonderful book entitled *The Grace of Yielding*. If only we would yield to God and seek wisdom from him each day. When I drive to my office in the morning, the one thing I ask God to give me is wisdom to help the couples I see. It does not matter how much knowledge one has about relationships; without wisdom there is no good way to use that knowledge.

Unfortunately, we have all become programmed to a microwave culture that looks for immediate gratification or change and encourages selfishness and pride, and that makes it difficult for us to walk in this Scripture. Some seem only to give in a marriage, and others seem only to take—not even realizing they are doing it. We can form new habits, one step at a time, that enables us to create an environment for healthier relationships. This is where the "couple's dialogue" I spoke of in the previous chapter creates the ability to have a safe space in a relationship where we can cultivate a deeper understanding of our partner.

## Unforgiveness Means the Shield of Faith is Down

Forgiveness creates the ability to put our shield of faith in place:

> Let all bitterness, wrath, anger, clamor and evil speaking be put away from you, with all malice. And be kind to one another, tenderhearted, forgiving one another, just as God in Christ also forgave you.
> —Eph. 4:29-32 NKJV

The only commandment Jesus gave to us was to love him and to love our brother. When we walk in kindness and love, we create a positive atmosphere that can allow us to energize our faith. To become the men and women God wants us to be in our marriages and other relationships, we must forgive as God forgives us.

Actually, the second letter to the Corinthians tells us that the only way we have the authority to tap into mighty weapons of God comes through being obedient to Jesus and his commandment of love. "For though we walk in the flesh, we do not war according to the flesh. For the weapons of our warfare are not carnal but mighty in God for pulling down strongholds, casting down arguments and every high thing that exalts itself against the knowledge of God, bringing every thought into captivity to the obedience of Christ, and being ready to punish all disobedience when your obedience is fulfilled" (2 Cor. 10:3-6).

I find in my therapy practice that when couples learn healthy ways of staying in adult-to-adult dialogue, connecting at a deeper, more intimate level, they create a deeper connection with each other. Meeting that ideal is difficult when people are in pain. It is like trying to exercise when our bodies are not in shape. When we are in pain in a relationship, it is so difficult to see through our partner's eyes. If we have built our whole emotional position on what we think is the reality, it is almost impossible to see what our partner is seeing from their perspective. But we don't have to give up our emotional position in the relationship to try to see our partner's position. Perhaps understanding that is the key to understanding true forgiveness.

I remember in the 1980s that I preached on the topic of forgiveness. That message would typically state that God says "I remember their sins no more," (NASB), and that he forgives us. Since this is what God does for us, we are to forgive and forget others. Then I had everyone stand and whisper the names of those they needed to forgive. Yet after the service, many people left still angry at the ones they just "forgave." I am afraid that is because what I told them to do is not what forgiveness really is. Our brain is like a computer with a lot of temp files. We cannot forget. God created our brains, so he knew we would not be able to do that. But we can move beyond the pain.

Sidney and Suzanne Simon in their book, *Forgiveness, How to Make Peace with Your Past*, developed the following ideas on forgiveness to reveal what it is not and what it is.[2]

When we are taught that forgiveness is forgetting, the pressure is on us to connect the two. God did not create and develop our brain to forget. Our brain is like a computer with temp files. What we can do through forgiveness is to move beyond the pain.

On certain occasions, when I am dealing with a couple where infidelity has occurred, I will ask Susan to join me in one of their sessions. It is sometimes helpful for couples to hear from her as how she dealt with the pain we had gone through. Not long ago, a wife asked Susan how she had gotten past what had happened in our marriage. Her answer was, "You don't forget it, you move beyond the pain so that you are able to forgive." Forgiveness is not letting someone off the hook. It is not saying that when we forgive we are saying that what they did was okay. That would only make things more difficult. When we forgive the hurt others have done to us, we are not absolving anyone of their sins. No one except God can do that. Rather, we are letting go of our emotions toward that individual—but that person still has to deal with the consequences of their behavior.

When we forgive we are not forcing ourselves to go through some form of "self sacrifice" throwing ourselves at the enemy to tolerate what was done to hurt us. What we don't need to do is to move toward forgiveness because someone told us we had to forgive that person who hurt us. I often tell couples not to forgive their partners just because I have brought up the topic in our counseling sessions. We need to be ready to forgive in our own time and place.

Forgiveness is not a clear-cut, one-time decision. We are so event-conscious in our culture. But I have found that forgiveness is an evolving journey of small steps preparing a heart to be able to forgive. In one sense I begin sowing the seeds of the idea of forgiveness in a person, sometimes long before they are ready.

I have seldom seen individuals able to move to forgiveness without first having a basic understanding of why someone inflicted hurt on them. The couples I see have deep hurts either from each other or from past wounds that have not healed. Simon and Simon stated that "forgiveness is a byproduct of an ongoing healing process." They wrote, "If you can learn how to heal those wounds, we usually find forgiveness as a gift at the end of the healing process when we no longer expect that person or our partner to pay for what they did."

In my experience, when one has a relationship with God it is far easier to move in the direction of forgiveness than it is for a person without that source of strength in their life. If we look at forgiveness as simply a religious obligation, and do not have the faith to operate in that type of obedience, few will be able to understand that concept. We would need to have a total understanding of unconditional love, and few humans know how to walk that out as Christ did for us.

If we look at forgiveness as a moral right (a right to stop being hurt by unfair situations), than an individual can create the environment for God to help them through the strength of the Holy Spirit to understand that forgiveness is the answer to moving forward and letting go of the negative energy in their lives.

The most profound revelation I have received in my own life is that when I forgive it is not for the benefit of the person who caused the pain, but rather it is for me. Forgiveness is something you do for yourself to let go of the negative energy that will suck the life out of you through bitterness. If I forgive someone who has died, it obviously isn't doing that person any good. But it does me a world of good. What robs us of the blessings in life is when we don't let go of our grudges and walk in unforgiveness. All of that negative energy will block us from being able to truly move forward and let go of the past.

When I work with couples, I very often see that many individuals have great difficulty forgiving their partner. It is never easy to forgive, and the thought of forgiving is not easy to swallow. In many situations, I can totally understand that. If it is part of the healing journey, then it makes sense that this will be difficult. But there are often situations when there is a more covert issue blocking an individual from forgiving. One of those is fear.

Many individuals who struggle with forgiveness have a fear that if they forgive they will become more vulnerable to being hurt again. That makes sense, but healing cannot happen without vulnerability. When a person has been deeply hurt one or more times by the same individual, that fear is going to be present unless that person can get in touch with their true selves and know that God wants to deliver that person from fear. The fear of becoming vulnerable can only be overcome when the individual learns to take back their personal power from the person who was responsible for inflicting the wound and move out of the victim stage toward healing and letting go of all those emotions that keep them stuck.

There are times when forgiveness and connecting with the person who hurt you does not happen at the same time. If forgiveness is a process, then the step of reconnecting with that person may be a process as well. A process, however, does not have to last a lifetime. Where infidelity has occurred in a marriage, forgiveness might be a decision followed by the process of walking out that forgiveness and learning to rebuild trust is a process that can follow that forgiveness.

Some people can navigate the stormy waters of forgiveness easily, while others have a difficult time. It is like grieving. In the grieving process, a person has to give themselves permission to feel sorrow. There is no set time for that process to be finished. The important thing is that we do not get stuck in a stage, like the victim stage mentioned above, and decide to stay there for a lifetime. That is when the root of bitterness can sink into our lives, and this can be very unhealthy, both physically and emotionally.

## When We Work Toward Healing–Forgiveness Just Happens

The three hardest tasks in the world are neither physical feats nor intellectual achievements. Instead, they are moral acts: to return love for hate, to include the excluded, and to say, "I was wrong." The following poem, in a paradoxical way, states both the result of unforgiveness and the blessing of forgiveness.

**Two Children**

Two children, a brother and a sister,
Born to a father who was a slave to wine.
They do remember their younger years of sorrow,
How their daddy used to hurt them time after time.

But somehow they grew to be so different.
Their lives turned out to be like day and night.
One lives in peace up in Ohio,
One was full of hate until she died.

I wondered what could make the difference in the two of them.
Both had reasons to be bitter.
But one was so sweet,
How could one live in peace and not the other?
Not long ago the answer came clear to me.

I saw the brother at his daddy's grave,
Placing flowers there his eyes were filled with tears
As he said, "Daddy once again I do forgive you
For the way you made us suffer through the years."

Now I can see how the two could be so different,
How their hearts turned out to be like day and night.
He lives in peace up in Ohio,
She was bitter till the day she died.
He lives in forgiveness up in Ohio,
She was bitter till the day she died.
A bitter heart was the reason that she died.
(Author Unknown)

Understanding what forgiveness really is, and why God considers it so important, will help us move through almost anything in our relationships that brings pain. This biblical principle is so important to keep those psychosocial stressors from causing even greater damage. Find

# SLAYING THE GIANT-KILLERS IN YOUR RELATIONSHIP

the wisdom in the Scriptures and stay away from a legalistic approach. Through the wisdom of God we can find the way to journey through forgiveness.

Here are some questions to ask yourself and journal:

1. In what way has God shown his forgiveness to you?

2. Why do you think forgiveness is so important in your relationship or marriage?

3. Can you remember an occasion when you received forgiveness from someone close to you that you did not deserve?

4. What do you think the pitfalls are if you don't resolve areas of unforgivness in your relationship?

5. Look at your own life to see if there are areas of unforgiveness. What are your plans to deal with these areas?

*Chapter Seven*

## AFTER THE AFFAIR

ONE AREA WHERE forgiveness is so difficult is infidelity. Because we are human and not God, forgiveness in some areas of our lives can be a daunting task. Our own story of recovering from infidelity is an example of grace and forgiveness. For Susan, my heart change paved the way for her journey of forgiveness. I could never do the kind of work I do, and I could never have written this book, if not for the repentance I went through and the heart change God gave me.

Much of my counseling practice deals with the aftermath of infidelity. It is possible that the pain of being betrayed may be even more painful than losing a loved one to death. Financial infidelity, emotional infidelity, and sexual infidelity are so difficult to repair. Still, I have seen miraculous healing in couples when both make a decision to heal each other and their relationship. Those who have been betrayed can never forget what happened, but they can move beyond their pain.

Rarely does an affair start because of sex. Instead, it usually starts with some sort of connection, which may be a friendly, smiling face drawing the person in. Few in an affair can accept that seventy-five percent of these relationships will fail because they are born out of lies, deception, and selfishness. It is true, but they are usually blind to that. The novelty of a person who is warm and connecting looks so much more attractive than whatever pain may be experienced in a current relationship. They are in the middle of the "love cocktail," but they are comparing apples to oranges. Often, years later—even if they do stay together—they come to my office because of trust issues. If they entered into an illicit relationship with each other before, why should they trust each other later?

*Why I Stayed* is a book recently written by Gayle Haggard. She is the wife of Ted Haggard, a prominent evangelical leader and the former pastor of a megachurch in Colorado. In 2006 he was caught soliciting sexual relations with another man. After being exposed, he had to leave the church, and Mrs. Haggard's account of her ordeal is a powerful and inspiring testimony to the power of forgiveness and grace.

When asked why she stayed, Gayle Haggard answered, "The first reason is that I really do love this man. And I know that he's more than any complication, flaw, and sin that he has committed. And the second reason is because of my faith." One can only imagine the stages of grief she went through. Her conclusion did not happen overnight, but it is a beautiful example of grace, forgiveness, reconciliation, and restoration.

Infidelity has always been an issue in our society. Affairs began to increase when women entered the workplace. According to Pat Carnes, the author of *Out of the Shadows: Understanding Sexual Addiction (1992)*, the recent dramatic rise in marital affairs resulted from the Internet and cybersex porn sites. He began doing work on sexual addiction in the 1980s and is today one of the leaders in the movement to heal sexual addiction. Carnes says a person who has serial affairs is probably dealing with sex addiction, as opposed to one who has a single affair. His Web site is www.sexhelp.com.

Affairs are often a symptom of a relationship problem. But this is not always the case. I am not suggesting that if there are relationship problems, an affair is justified. Too often we look at behavior and begin to judge. All I am saying is that usually people who have an affair first have a wound that increases their risk of making a very unwise and selfish choice. That individual usually has a character flaw. We could all agree that sex outside of marriage is sin, and the root cause of this behavior is rebellion toward a deeper relationship with God. But I have seen few Christian marriages get healed from the devastation of infidelity by just saying that one of the partners is in sin.

Facing the sin of infidelity is critical for remorse and repentance to occur. But there is still the healing between two individuals in the relationship—three individuals, if you look at the other person in the illicit relationship. Repentance does not undo the consequences of our sin. Repentance is a way of being remorseful, turning from our own self toward God, and learning divine wisdom for our lives. When we sow bad seed, we should expect a bad harvest. But just because we again start sowing good seed does not mean we will immediately get a good harvest, as we are still experiencing the bad harvest from the bad seed. As we continue sowing good seed, watering, fertilizing, and pulling the weeds out, we will eventually reap a good harvest.

Here is an unsettling statement: It is not in a human being's nature to be monogamous. We chose to be monogamous as a culture and as individuals. Without monogamy, we would experience chaos. Peggy Vaughan, the author of *The Monogamy Myth*, has great insight into this issue.[1] She writes, "No matter what reasons/excuses may be offered as to why someone has an affair, there is an essential 'trump card' that is necessary to proceed. In the final analysis (regardless of the reason for wanting to have an affair), acting on that desire ultimately depends on one thing: being willing to be dishonest and deceptive." Vaughn further states that "the future possibilities for the marriage are not determined by what happened in the affair; they are determined by what happens after the affair is known. Specifically, it is determined by the degree to which the one who had an affair is willing to be honest and answer all their spouse's questions about the affair."

## Thirteen Steps Leading to an Affair—and the Healing that can Come!

1. Individual problems and/or marital/relationship problems
2. Betrayal of the relationship through infidelity
3. The affair is discovered
4. A crisis develops in the relationship and family
5. All contact with the other person has to stop—usually a very difficult step
6. The betrayer shows signs of genuine remorse and repentance

7. Answering all questions (who, when, and where) and hanging in through the inevitable emotional turmoil
8. Seeking God's voice and trained professional counsel. Rarely can a couple be objective enough to repair the damage of infidelity by themselves.
9. Discovery of whether there is willingness to reconcile and heal. This requires dealing with a lot of opinions from family and friends. Most of those opinions overlook the reality that—with the beginning of remorse and forgiveness—most couples going through this horrible pain can heal
10. Rebuilding trust through developing a strategy to follow that path— primarily through actions, not just promises
11. Redeveloping the relational intimacy between the two individuals
12. Committing to develop a new honesty and to ongoing honest communication—a step most couples will find very difficult
13. The journey of forgiveness

Here are some reasons why those who have been betrayed may decide to see if they can heal their marriage or relationship:

1. Because he or she seems genuinely remorseful
2. Because there are kids involved
3. Because everyone deserves a second chance
4. Because alcohol is involved
5. He or she agrees to go to couple's therapy
6. The betrayed loves his or her partner and family
7. The betrayed almost strayed once
8. Because of faith and a relationship with God

Usually, many friends and family members will offer opinions about deciding to stay or return to a relationship. But advice from people with no relationship training are like those national opinion polls that survey people who have only opinions but no information to base them on. A marriage cannot be based on someone's opinion. Yes, we should seek wise, godly counsel. With wisdom in hand, forgiveness as a journey, and faith in what God wants for us, we can make a decision that can lead us to have the relationship of our dreams. Seek the Lord for a wise therapist who has a relationship with God and who has been trained to deal with these complex issues.

Regardless of whether the relationship survives, there will need to be a personal recovery from the emotional impact of discovering a betrayal. In her book *The Monogamy Myth,* Peggy Vaughan suggests these steps:[1]

1. Begin to accept that it happened and navigate through denial and blaming yourself. Even if there had been marital problems, the betrayer should have left or gotten a divorce before the selfish decision of infidelity was made.
2. Deliberately focus on dealing with it, not just trying to bury it.
3. Talk honestly about what happened. Overcome the secrecy about affairs.
4. Allow the time to heal. Time alone, however, is not enough. You won't be able to do this alone, but will need a trained, godly therapist.
5. Begin the journey of believing it is possible to recover—and that nothing is impossible with God.
6. Understand that this is not due just to your own failures, but that societal factors also play a part.

The individual who has been the unfaithful partner has a challenging journey if he or she wants to make amends. They must listen to their partner's anger over their discovery. With the shame it brings, it is difficult to hear a person's rage. But listening can be the most powerful part of healing. Often if the betrayed person is not able to express their pain as the other listens, they will usually implode from rage. If the individual is not able to vent, the anger will linger during the journey of grieving. That person will feel not only the pain of infidelity, but also the pain of their betrayer ignoring their pain and refusing to listen.

No one says it is easy. Be warned that a contemptuous style of communication kills. We cannot talk to our partner any way we want to and expect a great response—whether we are speaking to the person who has been unfaithful or the person who has been betrayed. Do not expect your partner to listen to your pain if the volume is loud. Try bringing the loudness of the sound down a little so your partner has no excuse not to listen.

The offender needs to spell out what he or she is sorry for, and the apology should be genuine and deep. An example of what I mean is, "I am sorry for the contempt I have shown you by being unfaithful." As I have seen many times in my office, simply saying "I'm sorry"—with no actions of remorse—will not be received. Most people need to see the action, not just hear it.

I hear lots of excuses. Some even accuse the person they betrayed! Somehow it was their fault. That is a great theory, but we are responsible for our own decisions. Many Christians try to blame Satan. The problem with that excuse is it enables us to shift blame away from our own carnality. You cannot cast out flesh.

When a couple comes into my office, I often ask the person who has been betrayed, "Why do you think your partner had an affair?" Seldom does that individual know why or how their partner could do that. Usually, after the person gets beyond their need to verbalize anger, they can finally have a dialogue about that issue. The person has usually just found out about the situation and is grieving a loss. Again, there is no timetable for grieving; it has to take its course. One of the stages is anger. I get concerned if the person gets stuck in the victim stage as I wrote in the previous chapter. That can lead to physiological issues that can affect not only their emotional health, but also their physical health.

If the couple is going to reconcile, at some point the journey of forgiveness will need to begin. Forgiveness is a transaction that takes two people who are willing to admit they are wrong. That journey—and earning any level of trust—will take a while. With forgiveness, remorse, and God's help, that journey can lead to an incredible relationship.

Most couples who try to heal their relationship after an affair have no plan in place to develop trust. Often the person who had the affair expects trust just to happen. When most couples try to do that on their own, without professional counseling, they will eventually hit a brick wall. I always ask the person who has been betrayed what they need from their partner to begin the journey of trust. Interestingly, they seldom know what they need.

People in this type of relationship should begin writing down in a journal what they need from their partner to develop trust again. Trusting will be a long process, but it has to begin somewhere. The partner who has betrayed can expect a certain resistance from the partner who has been betrayed to do the things needed to develop trust. But if the two of you don't do this, you will continue to question if another affair is going to happen. In the end, you probably won't make it.

An effective exercise for both individuals is to begin writing a list of what they need from their partner to gradually rebuild trust. From the point of view of the betrayed, the list might include requests such as telling me if you run into the person you had an affair with, giving me the itinerary for your travel, reducing overnight stays, telling me if you like my outfit or my hair, showing me some affection in other places outside the bedroom, and so on. Or from the point of view of the betrayer, the list could include letting me know when you are not sure of our relationship rather than making assumptions of what I am feeling or thinking, letting me know when you feel better about our future, telling me when you feel I have let you down, and so forth. This can be an evolving list and is a positive way to create a path to gradually rebuilding trust.

Although it has been many years since Susan and I reconciled, if a song or a television program comes on with infidelity as its theme, I will often ask Susan if she needs to talk about it. I choose to be proactive instead of reactive. In my office I will encourage men who have been unfaithful to do that. They are usually gripped by fear and don't want to upset the cart. Susan has never said she wanted to talk about it. Instead, she has said that she has moved beyond the pain. What I do is a gesture of care and love. I will never take for granted what we went through. A proactive strategy is a way for me to continue developing trust by showing I care.

As Janice Abrams Spring writes in her book, *After the Affair*, sometimes there is a need to take something apart to rebuild it in a stronger, more lasting way. A crisis can be a turning point where this rebuilding can happen. We can heighten our potential for change by being open to taking the marriage apart in order to strengthen it.

No one would wish the experience of infidelity on their worst enemy. But if it helps to uncover defects in the relationship, and grow as an individual and a partner, it may, in retrospect, seem worth it. As Carl Jung stated, "Seldom or never does a marriage develop into an individual relationship smoothly and without crisis. There is no birth of consciousness without pain."

When Susan left our marriage, that was the beginning of my true relationship with God—replacing the superficial one I had until then. I learned that life is a journey, not a harbor. With God as our source of strength, we can get in touch with our self, our true self, and reach our dreams in life by fulfilling the potential in all of us and in our marriages.

## Assumptions about Affairs that Often are True[2]

1. Affairs can be healed
2. An affair is usually an unconscious outcome—not a conscious decision to end the relationship
3. Both partners contribute to the rupture of the connection
4. Affairs reflect the intensity of the impulse to experience connection
5. Affairs offer the same opportunity for growth and healing as any other exit
6. All healing is best done in dialogue between the partners. With Imago Relationship Therapy, couples are taught how to have healthy dialogue to heal
7. Exits need to be closed (closed means closed). The individual must stop all communication and not see the person! Otherwise that will drain energy away from healing the relationship
8. A clear step-by-step process is imperative in healing affairs
9. Outside opinions and advice need to be minimized. This will just bring more confusion and less wisdom. Everyone has an opinion, and few of those are based on any training
10. A therapist must be active in guiding a couple through this process
11. A therapist must be highly conscious of their own opinions and biases

## Six Steps for Healing Relationship Affairs from an Imago Perspective

Healing a relationship after an affair is difficult, if not impossible, without the assistance of a professionally trained therapist. The therapist needs to be an individual who specializes in marital breakups. Not just any therapist will do. I am not saying that the Holy Spirit cannot heal a relationship where infidelity has occurred. I am saying that at times we are too damaged to be able to have the faith to believe that can occur. A trained Christian professional can blend both ideas and guide a couple to that healing. We are often not able to be objective enough to be able to tap into the spiritual issues. Our marriage was healed by the Holy Spirit but also by a trained professional in relationship therapy who gave us the tools to use.

Here are some steps to begin healing the damage of a broken marriage through the help of a trained Christian therapist. None is easy, and there will be a great deal of emotional energy to invest, much of it negative. Both partners need to be intentional about this journey and not let their emotions get the better of them.

1. The first step is for the partner who has been betrayed to express all the emotions they feel (grief, anger, rage, and so on) so they may be honored by the person who had the affair. A professional therapist can help both marriage partners take the trip across the bridge until all feelings are completely heard.
2. The second step is for the partner who had the affair to share their feelings. Without some level of equity in the dialogue, they will not be able to mirror what they are hearing from the partner who has been betrayed.
3. The third step is for the betrayed partner to ask any questions and get any information they want to know (who, when, where). The information should be general because very specific details will only cause more pain and will not help in the healing.
4. The fourth step is to use the couples dialogue (an Imago Relationship Therapy tool) to explore their relationship and to understand, validate, and own the things that happened that led to the affair.
5. The fifth step is for the partner who strayed to express remorse in a way that his or her partner can hear and accept. Remorse and repentance are mandatory for healing to happen.
6. In the sixth step the couple uses the Imago Relationship Vision Process tool to identify new symbols and new rituals

for a reconstituted marriage. This is a process where a couple co-creates a relationship vision of the relationship they truly want to guide them to develop their dream relationship where trusting each other is a priority.

I would say a very important seventh step is to seek God and ask him for the Holy Spirit who is our counselor and advocate and who gives us comfort to help us forgive and heal.

These steps to heal a broken marriage are essential to repair conflict. I often see couples who have had a long history of unresolved conflicts. A pattern of unresolved conflicts will eventually lead to major issues, but if this can be repaired when it happens, couples would not reach levels of despair and bitterness. If more couples would learn to face and repair their conflicts, I think infidelity would greatly diminish. For that matter, relationships would evolve to the level where safety and passion exist and they have the relationship of their dreams.

When couples fail to repair conflicts, they become disconnected and the sacred space between them becomes toxic. One major change in my marriage with Susan is how we try to repair conflicts as soon as they happen. Repairing the conflict—without trying to prove who is right—leads to harmony and connection.

*Chapter Eight*

# THE REST OF YOUR LIFE CAN BE THE BEST OF YOUR LIFE

> The thought manifests as the word; the word manifests as the deed; the deed develops into habit; and habit hardens into character. So watch the thought and its ways with care, and let it spring from love born out of concern for all beings.
>
> —Source unknown

A MIDDLE-AGED MAN came into my office seeking help with procrastination and not reaching his goals. Within the past twenty-four months, "Bill" had experienced the death of his wife, who was the love of his life, and also termination from a job where he had been very successful. As I listened to his story, I saw a man who was disillusioned with God due to all the loss he had experienced. He sat with his shoulders slumped, a dark cloud hanging over his head, and looked like he had been totally rejected. Bill had been unemployed for more than fourteen months in the midst of the worst recession our country has experienced since the Great Depression. A look of shame and unresolved hurt radiated from him. What could help this very talented individual?

Bill fidgeted with the paperweight on my desk and sighed. "After losing Margaret and my career so close together, I can't keep up with any of the regular routines of my life. I don't pay bills on time, my laundry is piled to the ceiling, and yard work is an afterthought. I still haven't found a job, and I'm not really looking all that hard. Everything feels meaningless since she died. Everything that mattered is gone. What's the point? How could God let this happen?"

As Bill spoke, he never looked up from the paperweight. If he had, he might have burst into tears. That might not have been a bad thing, but it just didn't fit his character.

I wanted to push some button that would make his loneliness and pain go away. But no such button exists. What he needed from me was validation and empathy—not sympathy or a Bible lesson. I find in my counseling that when I am too quick to pull out the Scriptures when one's heart is not ready, this can lead to shame. The counselee can feel they are not good enough, or that they have failed at the idea of God in their lives. He needed to move on, and to do that he was in for some hard work. You or someone you know might be in a similar situation.

Imagine reaching a peak in life. You are on a roll, celebrating your accomplishments and enjoying blessings and prosperity. Then you wake up one day and everything on this earth that mattered is gone. It would be like the air coming out of a beautiful balloon and seeing a crumpled pile of rubber in the middle of the living room. There is no way to inflate the balloon again, as it now has a gaping hole. Imagine the hopelessness Bill must have experienced. Imagine if something like this happened to you or to someone you love. Do you think it would affect your marriage and what you believed about yourself?

Bill started dating a woman, and from the beginning of this relationship they were having problems. Beginning to date was not the wisest thing to do during a time like this. He had much work to do to leave his baggage behind and resurrect his spirits. Yet his longing for connection was so powerful that it was difficult to avoid what we usually call a rebound experience. So he and I began the journey of helping him reinvent himself. He had to learn to become the right person before finding the right person. He had become bitter about life and his relationship with God. His heart had to change to enable him to rise above these circumstances.

His outlook reminded me of mine several decades earlier. What I learned from that journey was that faced with the truth about who we are, we often stay in denial. We remain in denial about words, deeds, and thoughts that reflect the character we bring to our marriage and

# THE REST OF YOUR LIFE CAN BE THE BEST OF YOUR LIFE

our life. That denial can undermine our best efforts to create a fulfilling, lasting marriage.

When one of my best friends informed me in 1978 that I was one of the most negative individuals he knew, I wanted to yell at him. At that point I wasn't exactly experiencing my brightest hour in life, and I certainly didn't need that put-down from a friend. I sat on a bench in front of the church I attended and asked myself if I was really that negative. When we are asked to face our demons, it is never easy. I was so angry at my friend that I wanted to scream. Then, there it was, a still small voice inside me saying "I told him to go to you and say that because of the call I have on your life." Two years before this happened, I was at the low point of my life and in deep depression. We were performing at a showroom in a big Miami, Florida, hotel. One night in despair and feeling hopeless, I had a .38 caliber gun in my mouth and just wanted to end my life. I remember thoughts of how selfish that would be to leave my six-year-old son fatherless. It was just a few months later that I would receive God into my life.

At first, I dismissed this message, but then I recognized that God was trying to get my attention. I had no idea how much my lack of self-awareness and all my baggage would affect my romantic relationship with Susan years later. Most of us fall in love without any perspective of what may come. Most people, including myself at that time, have no idea how our unfinished business or our internal dialogue can stop us from being successful.

So many times in my life, God had been trying to get my attention. So many times I refused to listen. Being inquisitive about my friend's statement that I was a negative person, I asked for an appointment with one of the pastors. He counseled me to begin a journey that would have been much shorter, except for my own stubbornness. I know I am far from the only person that has ever happened to. If only we weren't so bullheaded; if only we were more teachable. I started learning how to go from being a professional pessimist to a trained optimist.

> A pessimist is one who makes difficulties of his opportunities and an optimist is one who makes opportunities of his difficulties.
> —Harry Truman

At this point you might be asking, what does my journey from negativity have to do with love, marriage, and relationships? If we don't believe in ourselves, how can we believe in a lasting, romantic love relationship with another person? There has to be an "I" for there to be a "we."

Part of developing relational skills is to get in touch with our true self—the original creative energy and the potential that God intended for us. This requires us to take responsibility for how we sabotage relationships with a partner. We need to stop hurling all blame, all shame, and all guilt at our partner—and discover how to get in touch with the potential we have as human beings. When we are reactive to our romantic partner, it is usually because some of our own unfinished business has been triggered, not because our partner is trying to hurt us.

## Overcoming the Fear of Failure and the Fear of People

No matter how much work, how much participation, and how much prayer and effort goes into our dreams, it still seems that great victory in our marriages, our finances, our careers, and our spirituality involves elements of faith, nerve, and courage. To attain these goals requires more than merely sitting in my prayer closet waiting for my prayers to be answered. Rather, to attain these goals requires an action, an element of faith, and the courage to step out in faith.

Joshua 1:8 reads, "This Book of the Law shall not depart from your mouth, but you shall meditate in it day and night, that you may observe to do according to all that is written in it. For then you will make your way prosperous, and then you have good success" (NKJV). This Scripture is saying that we first need to stay in God's Word and walk in that Word. But we still have to take a step of action, a step of faith to implement our dreams in life. Notice that "you will make your way prosperous, and then you will have good success." The scripture doesn't say God will make your way prosperous.

Psychologist Herbert Otto says, "Change and growth take place when a person has risked himself and dares to become involved with experimenting with his own life." To experiment with one's own life is very exhilarating, joyful, happy, and wondrous—and also frightening.

# THE REST OF YOUR LIFE CAN BE THE BEST OF YOUR LIFE

This journey requires our learning how to get over our fear of failure and our fear of people. These two fears begin in childhood from the messages we hear. These messages form our "internal dialogue"—that inner voice that says "we can't" instead of "we can." I have used these principles to transform myself from a professional pessimist to a trained optimist. As we heal the shame that binds us, we can step into our potential and reach our dreams.

## When You Look into the Mirror, What Do You See?

Decades ago I heard Doug Weade teaching at an Amway convention. He was teaching on the story of Gideon in the Bible. Those ideas were so instrumental in helping me become an optimist. I decided to take a new look at some of those principles and merge them with my ideas on becoming the individual God wants us to become. Remember, when we are secure in our own self, we will be a better partner in a relationship.

There is a story of a young Israeli in the sixth and seventh chapters of the book of Judges. It is a fascinating account of learning to take a negative experience and changing it to a positive one. Israel was dominated by an interesting people called the Midianites. These people were unruly and cruel. There were none like them in history. They had a stone-age mentality. They sacrificed their first-borns to stone statues; they burned them alive in wild orgies. They hauled off children from conquered countries and used them as sex slaves in these orgies.

The Midianites were nomads. They were lousy farmers and lousy merchants, but they were born warriors. They dominated the Middle East for a season, like a little ball in a pinball machine going from one kingdom to the next. They practiced a scorched-earth policy, much as the Germans did in World War II. When they came to Israel, they hauled off their children, consumed their wine and crops, poisoned their wells, burned their fields, and murdered the elderly and "useless."

Every seven years, Israel would crawl out and start over. Eventually, they got tired of starting over. As they looked everywhere, they could see camels, warriors, campfires, and tents. Finally God sent an angel to visit a nobody farm boy named Gideon. Far from being a hero, Gideon said that out of all Israel his tribe is the least, and out of the whole tribe his family is the least, and out of the whole family he was the least. "Oh Lord, how can I deliver Israel? Behold, my clan is the poorest in Manasseh, and I am the least in my father's house" (Judg. 6:15 AMPLIFIED).

Gideon couldn't even support a wife and family. He had an old abandoned winepress where he hid things. As he was darting from rock to rock to go to his wine press, an angel of the Lord stood under a great oak tree and saluted him as if he were a five-star general. The angel said, "Hail mighty man of valor. The Lord is with you." Imagine if that had happened to you—God coming to you and saying, "Hail mighty man or woman of valor." Gideon must have thought he was hallucinating.

Then Gideon asked one of the most profound questions about life and God. "O sir, if the Lord is with us, why is all this befallen us? And where are all His wondrous works of which our fathers told us, saying, Did not the Lord bring us up from Egypt? But now the Lord has forsaken us and given us into the hand of Midian" (Judg. 6:13 AMPLIFIED). In other words, if God is with us, why ...? Why do the Midianites steal our children, poison our water, and kill our parents? Why year after year? If God is with us, and this happens year after year, what would it be like if he wasn't with us?"

Humanity's big question is if God is with us, why do orphans starve on the streets of Calcutta, why do we have cancer, why do we have poverty, why do we have hatred, why do we have heartbreak? Why do the innocent die? Why do the Midianites dominate us, kill us, and haul us off?

What was God's response? Did he answer Gideon's questions? No. "Then the LORD turned to him and said, 'Go in this might of yours, and you shall save Israel from the hand of the Midianites. Have I not sent you?'" (Judg. 6:14 NKJV). God told Gideon to go in his own power and seize his country back. He didn't explain the suffering, and he didn't explain what was happening. It wasn't an explanation at all, but it was an answer.

> Why do we have cancer?—Find a cure! Why do we have poverty?—Change it! Why do we have a bad marriage?—Heal it! Why do we have fears and habits that block love? "Go in your power and seize your country!" Seize the true self God created in you and that he longs to have you bring to your life and your marriage.

This is what God said to a nobody farm boy who was not even a private in the army, let alone a general. Nevertheless, God told him to *go*! Don't pray and fast for three months as an excuse not to act. Just do it. I am not saying there is no time for praying and fasting. Yet God told Gideon not to wait but to go and make it happen. And I think he is telling us the same thing. We need to trust in who God created us to be. If we do, we won't live in fear.

## Three Keys to Success, Favor, and Prosperity in Life and in Your Relationships

### Key One: Work in Action

You have got to give something to get something. Some people work themselves silly, yet they don't succeed and prosper. It is true we cannot succeed without work. But many people work hard and still go nowhere, so hard work alone is not the only ingredient. An individual who digs ditches works hard. We need to learn to work smarter, not just harder.

God told Gideon to go, move, act, pick up the phone, keep it going, and keep on keeping on. The historian Arnold Toynbee said life is not a harbor; life is a voyage. President Ford, when asked how he moved through crowds, replied, "I keep moving." If we do not give our lives, our marriages, or our relationships something, if we do not plant something or put anything in, we will never get anything back.

### Key Two: God-Reliance and Self-Reliance

*Go in your own power.* This was an incredible statement to make to a nobody farm boy with low self-esteem. If Gideon had looked in the mirror, he would have seen nothing. In the movie, *Oh God*, with George Burns and John Denver, God said, "Go use your talents to solve the American dollar." Denver's character replied, "I can't even balance my own checking account."

Self-reliance tells us to quit waiting until you have enough education, quit waiting until you have the right contacts, quit waiting until you move into a different neighborhood, and quit waiting until you buy it or sell it. You have what you need right now. Do you want permission to succeed? Okay! You have it. You hereby have permission to succeed.

The number-one principle to success in life and marriage is self-reliance by meditating in the Word of God and activating your faith and stepping out in faith—not reliance on your fearful self of old habits, but on the true self that God has created you to become. Look at Jesus feeding the five thousand (which was probably more like fifteen thousand when you add the women and children). There they were. Three days in the hills with no toilets, no canned foods, no Big Macs, no police force, and no hospital. It took just three days for the disciples of Jesus to panic.

Jesus said, "Feed them." Do not talk to me about the past seven years. Change your old self, change your marriage, change your career, change your country, and change your church. Jesus said, "Feed them."

The disciples said, "What are we going to feed them with?"

Jesus said, "You are going to feed them with food."

The disciples said, "How are we going to feed them?"

Jesus said, "You don't have anything?" The disciples said, "Well, we might have something." They came back with fish and bread.

They said, "What is this among so many?"

Jesus fed them—and had twelve baskets left!

God says to us, "You already have it." When you think you cannot go on anymore, you need to remember that you already have it—with twelve baskets left. We need to think big, think bigger, dream bigger. So big that God must play a part for it to happen within yourselves, your families, and your lives.

Start seeing your marriages as whole and healed. Start seeing yourself living up to your true potential, and start seeing your dreams realized. Then we can go in our own power and seize our "country"—and God will be with us. Multiply your dream times God, and there is no telling what you will accomplish.

## Key Three—Self Worth

You have to believe in the face in the mirror. You have got to get free from the guilt, greed, ugliness, and shame that fuels those crippling fears of failure and of people. Shame is the root of our fears, and shame is fueled by fear. The message *shame* brings is:

# THE REST OF YOUR LIFE CAN BE THE BEST OF YOUR LIFE

**S**hould
**H**ave
**A**lready
**M**astered
**E**verything

Our internal dialogue from childhood can bring shame into our minds. We need to heal the shame that binds us and keeps us from reaching our potential, the shame that binds us from bringing ourselves wholeheartedly to our relationships.

The Bible says that the fear of man brings something with it: "The fear of man brings a snare" (Prov. 29:25 NKJV). A good snare, if it is balanced properly, is designed to work with you. Any tug or pull tightens the snare. Once you are in it, any attempt to get out only tightens its grip.

Once you allow a personality or group of people to dictate how you will live your lives, once you start on that treadmill, you are in for a disillusioning experience. Why? Galatians chapter five says if we fail to live up to the standard that people set for us, they will despise us. But it also says that if we succeed in living up to the standard people set for us, they will despise us anyway. In verse eleven, the apostle Paul said, "And I, brethren, if I still preach circumcision, why do I still suffer persecution?" (NKJV) Paul also said, "For in Christ Jesus neither circumcision nor uncircumcision avails anything, but faith working through love" (5:6 NKJV). You are not going to please them no matter what car you drive. If we learned to live up to their standard, they would just change the standard. The solution comes in the last two verses of Galatians five: "If we live in the Spirit, let us also walk in the Spirit. Let us not become conceited, provoking one another, envying one another" (5:25-26 NKJV).

We spend ninety percent of our time trying to please people who could care less and ten percent of our time pleasing the people who really love us. Take that and apply it to your marriage. Try spending ninety percent of your time (instead of ten percent) meeting your partner's needs. What would your return be? Galatians 5:25 says to let the Holy Spirit be your guide in all you say and do. When God sent his angel to Gideon, Gideon was just a farm boy who looked like a big zero. God said to the angel, "When you look at him, show him respect." Why? "In three weeks that young man will lead three-hundred men to destroy the greatest war machine the world has ever seen. That nobody farm boy is a conqueror, a mighty man of valor."

## The Difference in what God Sees in Us and what We see in Ourselves

What do you see when you look in the mirror? Shame? Fear? An old habit? Or the true self within us? There was a thirteen-year-old French girl who was at school when one day she slammed her history book shut and went home. That girl was Joan of Arc. When she looked at herself, she didn't see anything. But God saw a fifteen-year-old girl in armor on a white charge leading her country into a victorious battle. God said, "You have it. Seize your country." Just try telling Joan of Arc that you are too young, that you have to wait. You've got it now.

Tell a sixty-three-year-old man who lived in central Kentucky and made $124,000 with a restaurant. In two years the federal government would redirect traffic from the highway where his restaurant was located onto an interstate. Almost bankrupt, he sold out. He said, "What did I do, God? How could you allow a government bureaucracy to ruin me?" He looked in a mirror and saw nothing. But God saw something. The man began to hear voices that said, "You've got it, old man." With a Social Security check of $110 a month, a pressure cooker, and a 1957 Chevy, he began peddling Kentucky Fried Chicken franchises. The man's name was Harland Sanders. When he started, he didn't have the money to rent a motel room, so he slept in his car. Try convincing Col. Sanders that you are too old to make it. God saw a man who had potential if he could overcome the fear of failing.

Tell Stephen Hawking you don't have enough to make it. He is in a wheelchair. The only energy he has is to lift his head off his chest. Others would not see much in looking at Stephen Hawking, but God saw a man with great potential.. The September 4, 1978, issue of *Time* magazine said that Hawking "is regarded as the premier scientist of the twentieth century." He has to remember everything because he cannot write it down. He was like Mozart with a symphony in his head. Tell Stephen Hawking you don't have enough. Unfortunately, as is so often

# THE REST OF YOUR LIFE CAN BE THE BEST OF YOUR LIFE

true with others, Stephen Hawking is an example of a man who does not recognize the miracle God has done for him. Recently he has publicized anti-God statements. But I use him to illustrate how God can work miracles in our lives and we still reject him.

A young Illinois statesman looked in a mirror. All he saw was a failure. He heard voices too, but how could he believe them? In the mirror he saw a haggard man who had just lost his biggest gamble. He had a lot of failures:

1831—Failed in business
1832—Failed when he ran for state legislature
1833—Tried another business venture and failed
1835—His girlfriend died and he had a nervous breakdown. When the doctors put him in bed, they told him not to get out. He got out to fail again
1837—Ran for public office again—and failed
1838—Ran for speaker of the house—and failed
1840—Failed when he ran for the U.S. Congress
1842—Ran for the U.S. Congress and won his second victory. Up for re-election, with all the advantages of the incumbency, he ran again and failed
1848—He retired from politics
1858—A bunch of wheeler-dealers convinced him he should make one more try. He thought he could do it. He had a lot of vision, a lot of wit and humor, and a big burden. He thought he was the right man for the job

He gambled every dime and every friend's dime and ran for the U.S. Senate. But he failed. He looked in the mirror and saw a bankrupt loser and heard a voice say, "Go in your own power and seize your country." God saw that Abraham Lincoln was to become one of the greatest presidents to lead our country. In 1860, he became the president to lead our country through the Civil War.

Fear of people. How is that handled? Fear of failure. How is that handled? We "go in our power and seize our country!" How is that done? Scripture's answer is found in the writing of the apostle Paul, inspired by the Holy Spirit. Paul's answer to the fear of failure is to fail. (That does take a lot of worry out of it.) To be precise, Paul teaches us to die. He says the best way to live is to die. In Philippians 1:21 Paul writes, "For to me, to live is Christ, and to die is gain" (NKJV).

In *The Truth About Love,* Pat Love says it is the relationship that sustains the husband and wife as they fall in and out of love with each other over the years of their marriage. She advises, "Don't ask what is good for you and me, but ask what is good for the relationship." Couples will succeed as they reach that level of maturity. So Paul has a great principle for relationships. Be willing to fail or die for the relationship. That is not an easy concept, as I wrote earlier in this book. We have all been programmed in a selfish culture. We bring ten percent of us to our spouse, to our dreams—and we trap ninety percent in the snare of fear and shame.

I understand this is not an easy place to reach. But as we discussed in the *Liposuction of Your Soul* chapter, if we go to the next level in our relationship with God, and then go to the deeper level of connection with our spouse, we can achieve this advanced level of maturity.

The fear of failure keeps us from even trying. It even keeps us from ever starting. It is one thing to dream and another to build. It is not the fear of failure; it is the fear of people. What they think. It is the fear of rejection.

As the comic strip character Pogo said, "We have met the enemy—and he is us." It is not people who are the barrier, but our shame and fear of disapproval and rejection. If we apply Paul's formula for success from Philippians 3:12 to reach for the prize. "Not that I have already attained, or am already perfected; but I press on, that I may lay hold of that for which Christ Jesus has also laid hold of me" (NKJV). We need to get hold of whatever it was that God saw in us.

Paul continues: "Brethren, I do not count myself to have apprehended; but one thing I do, forgetting those things which are behind and reaching forward to those things which are ahead, I press toward the goal for the prize of the upward call of God in Christ Jesus" (Phil. 3:13-14 NKJV). I am going to get in touch with my true self. We should also forget the past and reach out and grab tomorrow. Pressing toward the goal for the prize, for the high calling, is seizing our true self. This formula can provide the momentum to carry us through. I do, however, know how difficult it may be to "forget the past" when there are unresolved conflicts from our past that have deeply wounded us. Perhaps what really needs to happen is forgiveness and making peace with the past so that we can go forward unencumbered with negative baggage.

Get a sense of your own destiny and your relationship's destiny. Eventually you will have to be forgiven and forgive. You cannot hold it against yourself forever. Ask this: Why did Jesus pick me if I am so bad? From your true self, you can let go of the fear and shame that builds walls in your relationships.

Long before we ever existed, God chose us. God chose me. And he chose you. Find out what he sees. Philippians says, "Finally, brethren, whatever things are true, whatever things are noble, whatever things are just, whatever things are pure, whatever things are lovely, whatever things are of good report . . . meditate on these things" (4:8 NKJV). If we could begin focusing on affirmations and positives in our partner, where would we be? With almost every couple I counsel, there is always something positive they can acknowledge about each other. It may be difficult at first, especially if one is in pain, but we can all stretch and begin to see where it will take us. And it will take us far, for we can have the life, relationship, and marriage we are destined to have.

## The Key to Prosperity is Favor, Not Money

The goal here is to begin seeking and praying for *favor*, and that will bring us our dreams. As Scripture says,

> Let not mercy and truth forsake you; bind them around your neck, write them on the tablet of your heart, and so find favor and high esteem in the sight of God and man. Trust in the Lord with all your heart, and lean not on your own understanding; in all your ways acknowledge Him, and He shall direct your paths.
> —Prov. 3:3-6 NKJV

> A good name is to be chosen rather than great riches, loving favor rather than silver and gold.
> —Prov. 22:1 NKJV

These are some of my favorite motivational statements. I suggest putting them on index cards to remember:

- If you want something you never had, you have to do something you have never done
- Get a clear sense of direction. Know where you are going
- Do what you love; what you love will reward you
- Commit your life to excellence
- Dedicate yourself to lifelong learning. Learn and grow
- Success is the outcome of a focused life
- If you don't like what you are reaping, change what you are sowing
- Get around the right people who are at the next level
- Persistence—never give up
- It is not my responsibility; it is my response to his ability

## Don't Panic

One foundational biblical principle has to be part of our walk when we decide to step into our true self and overcome the fear of failure and fear of people. That principle is found in Proverbs chapter sixteen: "Roll your works upon the Lord [commit and trust them wholly to Him; He will cause your thoughts to become agreeable to His will, and] so shall your plans be established and succeed" (16:3 AMPLIFIED).

One night a few years ago I was in a deep sleep. I had been feeling a little nervous about the economy and how it would affect Susan and me. (Little did I know that our country was heading into a serious recession.) Deep in this sleep somewhere far off I thought I heard my name being called. I disregarded this at first. Yet it continued calling, "Johnny, Johnny." As I slowly woke up, drowsy at first, I thought it was my mother, who always called me Johnny. But I quickly realized she had died a couple of years before. Then I thought my wife had called me. But she was in a deep sleep, so it could not have been her. I then realized the voice had to be God. So I went out to our family room

# THE REST OF YOUR LIFE CAN BE THE BEST OF YOUR LIFE

and opened up my Bible and devotional book. How often do we wake up in the night and then lay a prisoner in our bed trying to go back to sleep. Often that time is a creative time to get up and go write or read or meditate on God's Word. My mind is usually free of stress or other chatter from life at times like those, so I have learned to step out when that happens.

The devotional I was using at the time was *Faith to Faith*, by Kenneth and Gloria Copeland. The devotion for that day was titled "Don't Panic." It started by stating, "Right now you may be on the edge of a major decision . . . about to make a change in your job or your church or your personal life. You know, you need divine guidance. And you're hoping desperately to hear from the Lord. If that is your situation, don't panic." The Scripture to go with this was Proverbs 16:3: "Roll your works upon the Lord [commit and trust them wholly to Him; He will cause your thoughts to become agreeable to His will and] so shall your plans be established and succeed" (AMPLIFIED).

No matter what decision we make about our marriage, our career, or our children, we need to develop the ability to roll those issues upon the Lord, energize our faith, and trust him so that we can gradually develop our thoughts into his will. Our trust is not in our paycheck. It is not in what we are seeing, feeling, or hearing. Our trust is in the Lord. When we trust in the Lord we receive his favor, and the key to prosperity is favor, not money. With trust in God we can walk in wisdom and prudence and rely on him to influence our thought process when we are making major decisions.

The Bible says that God will direct our paths. All we have to do is learn to listen to him, even in the year of the drought, and he will meet our needs: "For God has not given us a spirit of fear, but of power and of love and of a sound mind" (2 Tim. 1:7 NKJV). To learn to trust God, we must feed on his Word daily. This is a journey, not an event.

The next time you feel like God can't use you, just remember:

Noah was a drunk
Abraham was too old
Isaac was a daydreamer
Jacob was a liar

Leah was ugly
Joseph was abused
Moses had a stuttering problem
Gideon was afraid
Sampson was a womanizer
David had an affair and was a murderer
Elijah was suicidal
Isaiah preached naked
Jonah ran from God
Naomi was a widow
Job went bankrupt
John the Baptist ate bugs
Peter denied Christ
The disciples fell asleep while praying
Martha worried about everything
The Samaritan woman was divorced multiple times
Zaccheus was too small
Paul was too religious
Timothy had an ulcer
and
Lazarus was dead!

No more excuses! God can and will use you to your full potential—if you let him. Besides, we are not the message—we are just the messengers. He is calling us to go into our own power and seize the country of our true self, of wholehearted marriage, and of a life lived from his power rather than from fears, shame, and the old habits they fed.

So, I invite you to consider the following:

In childhood, what did you like to do? What did you do well?

In adolescent years, what did you like to do? What did you do well?

In adult years, what do you like to do? What do you do well?

# THE REST OF YOUR LIFE CAN BE THE BEST OF YOUR LIFE

Write down your answer to the following:

What would be your dream if you knew you wouldn't fail?

What would you dream if you took fear out of it?

What is your dream?

To have a dream, whether a career dream, a relational dream, or a parenting dream, we have to have a burning desire—and that can only come from faith. Faith is energized action. Faith comes by hearing the Word. When we hear the Word out loud, that power permeates into our brains and activates our faith. Then that faith requires an action. What gets in the way of that energized action is reason—and sometimes reason is the guillotine of faith. What I mean by reason is when we look at a faith step in the natural and go by feelings, we probably won't take it because we will let fear get in the way. But if we let our spirit man dominate our natural man, then we tap into the treasures God has for us. If we want to be giants in the kingdom of God, we need do what ninety percent of the body of Christ does not do.

Let the words and deeds of faith become your habits and your character. Seize the self God created in you. In that power, bring your "true self" fully to your life, your relationship, and your marriage. Shatter the walls of fear and shame. Claim what God has created you to be. You will see that anything is possible.

*Chapter Nine*

## IS REAL LOVE OR VINTAGE LOVE POSSIBLE?

THEY WERE A young, attractive couple sitting across from Susan and me in a Starbucks™ in Boise, Idaho. Her eyes looked into his so intensely that I could feel the energy across the room. Her long blonde hair fell softly on her shoulders. Her feet rubbed his under their table. He held her hand, softly stroking her thumb as he looked into her eyes. This is what love looks like. As a marriage therapist, I notice these things.

I pushed myself out of my seat and walked across the room. So they wouldn't think I was a nut, I introduced myself and my profession and said to them, "Your look of love has such an intense energy that it fills this room, I had to come over to tell you both what a positive experience you are sharing."

With a red face she told me, "We just got engaged this morning, and I guess it is showing." I then went back to the table with Susan. Of course, Susan never ceases to be amazed at my spontaneity. This couple was much like Susan and me at the beginning of our relationship. When that love cocktail hits, we think these feelings will last forever. We have all heard and seen other couples with that same glow of romance.

There is an attachment crisis in our culture. For many couples, Christian or not, the idea of real love and a long-term marriage is difficult to imagine. In this decade couples are waiting longer and longer to get married—if they do decide to marry. More and more couples are living together without getting married. Children are being born into unwed situations, and those children will probably never experience their biological parents marrying. This is what we are handing down to the next generation. Will the institution of marriage survive?

Some research shows that marriages are surviving in spite of the attacks on the institution. My wife and I went from being incredibly in love, to destroying each other, to infidelity, to restoration, to reconciliation—and then to the relationship of our dreams. I know it is possible to achieve this.

Recently a young man came into my office needing to share a secret he had kept from his wife for more than fifteen years. He felt the way they had come together and gotten married was not based on him loving his wife. He did not know what love was supposed to begin with, and he did not have any role model to know what love looks like. The young man was now rationalizing his marriage, which is something people do when they no longer feel the sizzle.

It is possible that a relationship does not live up to one's understanding of what love is. And it possible that the problem might not be with the relationship itself. Instead, the problem might be what your image of love is. Whatever our thoughts are about the relationship, is it possible that the difficulties lie not in our partner, but in our unrealistic expectations about love? Janet Abrams Spring writes in her book *After the Affair* what some of those expectations might be. Here are a few of them:

- My partner and I should feel a deep, unspoken bond at all times
- My partner should be able to anticipate my needs
- I should not have to work to be trusted
- A good marriage is free of conflict
- If I am not happy in my relationship, it is my partner's fault
- We should not have to work at feeling sexual desire for each other; it should come naturally or not at all
- When passion dies, so does the relationship

In part, as I wrote earlier, our expectations of love come partially from the programming we receive through our culture. Part of that is what we see in movies and on television. We are programmed by our microwave culture with its instant everything, including instant gratification. Even our notions about a sexual relationship are based on what we see in the mass media. For couples married for decades, the need to find a Hollywood sizzle can be disappointing. But does this mean we cannot have a deep, romantic relationship over decades? I believe we can enjoy a lasting relationship that is profoundly romantic and passionate. Susan and I found that through intentional discovery and continuing the journey I have been writing about. The Hollywood style of relationships is simply not the design that the Lord has for us in a godly marriage.

Here is one version of an intimate bond taken from a book by Cheryl Mercer called *Grown Ups*. This is what I believe a "real love" relationship looks like. It is sober, profound, and mature.

> When I think about marriage, what I long for most, strangely enough, is not an elevated spiritual union with a man; that's a fantasy not readily envisioned. What seems wondrous to me instead are the small, shared rituals that bind a man and woman in familiar intimacy, the borders inside which they love, choose furniture, plan vacations, quarrel over closet space, share the toothpaste, celebrate Christmas the same way they did last year. I've been in love myself, so I know something of what it's like to build a life together—the private jokes, the friends you share, knowing in advance which of you makes the coffee and which goes for the paper, even the comfortable tedium of hearing his or her favorite story yet again. To promise to share forever the small—not only the grand—moments of life seems to me profoundly human, more intimate even than making love with someone for the first time.

There are couples who have a long-term marriage, like my mother and father who were married for sixty-five years. This type of marriage is what we need to see and expect when we fall in love and decide to get married. Unfortunately, those expectations are what we look for and then get disappointed when the fireworks are no longer there. At that point, many individuals start thinking they are not in love anymore. How sad!

The problem is that we invest more time and attention in preventative maintenance for our cars than for our marriages. The two most important things we do in life are the two we invest in the least: marriage and parenting. As I mentioned earlier, most churches are not doing a good job in responding to this issue. A token message on marriage and the occasional marriage seminar is generally what the church is doing. The seminars are usually experiences for marriage enrichment with lectures and note taking.

Marriage conferences need to be experiential. When the conference is experiential, couples can learn important skills. Unfortunately, that is not enough to counter the prevailing winds in the larger culture which include temptations and negativism.. Only when the church becomes intentional about helping marriages become healthy will there be a change.

When couples fall in love and gradually descend into a power struggle, they lose hope. Remember, conflict is growth trying to happen. The good news is that there can be a transformation from the power struggle to real love—vintage love. Making that transformation, however, requires educating ourselves on healthy relationships. There are some wonderful books with great information like *The Truth About Love, How To Improve Your Marriage Without Talking About It, Getting the Love You Want, Keeping the Love You Find,* and many more. Many books do what I am trying to do in *Rebuilding Broken Bridges*: helping readers understand how a marriage breaks down, the ways to begin the journey toward healing the rupture, and keeping the sacred space between two individuals safe and devoted, rather than toxic.

Couples can also focus on what a godly marriage looks like. There is no reason a godly marriage cannot be romantic and passionate and safe. I know that is what God intended, and the Old Testament's Song of Solomon is the proof of that.

The following are some concepts I have discovered to help develop a picture of what a godly marriage and family can be. These concepts do not constitute a Hollywood picture of marriage, but rather a biblical style of finding a godly marriage. Again, a godly marriage can be a deep, romantic relationship where we can gaze into each other's eyes, flirt, and be playful. We can have a Christian marriage that is full of fun. A godly marriage that is safe and secure will create fun and romance. No one has to give that up.

## Characteristics of a Godly Marriage and Family

Most Christians think of their church and their Christian walk much like a cafeteria. They go when they want to, scan the menu, select what they want, eat the food, pay for what they eat, get up, and leave. Then they wonder why they are not receiving the blessings that a godly home can bring. I do not want to promote the idea that church attendance is the key to a great marriage. The difference comes in being not just a Sunday-morning Christian, but a seven-day-a-week Christian. The key is not churchgoing or observing religious events, but rather starting a journey of life to be connected to God. Assimilate these ideas on the characteristics of a godly marriage and family, but remember: Take one step at a time. Otherwise, we may feel like we have failed if we are not able to put them into place.

All the research on how children are affected by divorce and by growing up in a fatherless home suggests that families in our country are in the state of disarray. And it is no wonder. I believe that when men take their rightful position in the family that that is when the family can have true blessings. This is an important step toward a complete marriage, one that is safe and passionate. Research has shown us that men come into a relationship by how they perform, and these steps can help accomplish that. In my counseling I have noticed that wives find a godly man very attractive; they feel safe and secure with that type of man.

## The First Basic Ingredient for a Godly Family is Fatherhood

> For this reason [seeing the greatness of this plan by which you are built together in Christ], I bow my knees before the Father of our Lord Jesus Christ, for Whom every family in heaven and on earth is named [that Father from Whom all fatherhood takes its title and derives its name].
> —Eph. 3:14-15, Amplified

This Scripture is a treasure, especially when you look at the original Greek of the New Testament. The word *family* is derived from the word *father* in the original language. The Greek word for father is *patri,* and the Greek word for family is *patria.* This Scripture in Ephesians is saying that the Father is the life source of the Trinity (Father, Son, and Holy Spirit), and that the father is also to be the life source of the family on earth. Father is the ultimate name of God in heaven, and the secret to security in the family lies with the human father. This is even true of the relation between Jesus the Son to his Father. Many Christians pray to Jesus, but we should remember that he said, "I am the way, the truth, and the life. No one comes to the Father except through Me" (John 14:6 NKJV). God the Father in the heavenly realm is the model of what a father should be in the earthly realm. The father being the life source of the family was the original design, but we have gotten it out of order.

The couples I work with often have a core wound of rejection. The Father is the key to responding to that wound. In John 15:16–17 Jesus says, "You have not chosen Me, but I have chosen you and I have appointed you [I have planted you], that you might go and bear fruit and keep on bearing, and that your fruit may be lasting [that it may remain, abide], so that whatever you ask the Father in My Name [as presenting all that I AM], He may give it to you. This is what I command you: that you love one another" (AMPLIFIED BIBLE). The good news is that you have been chosen by the Father.

I wrote earlier that if we have insecure attachments in childhood, we tend to have insecure attachments in our adult love relationships. But when we have secure attachments in childhood, we tend to have secure attachments in our adult love relationships. The godly father is the cure for rejection. Conversely, a father who does not model love but instead models shame, will raise his children to be in some ways his mirror image. A godly father is not a perfect father—we are not Jesus, and we have to learn how to love unconditionally. Only Jesus, the Son of God, was able to do that.

## The Father as Priest, Prophet, and King

> Wives, submit to your own husbands, as to the Lord. For the husband is head of the wife, as also Christ is head of the church; and He is the Savior of the body. Therefore, just as the church is subject to Christ, so let the wives be to their own husbands in everything."
> —Eph. 5:22-24 NKJV

Over the years, many have taken this Ephesians Scripture to mean that a wife is to submit to her husband since men are the head, or king, of the house. But the word *submit* really means humility expressed in love and service—and not lording over the family and wife as slaves. At first, I wanted to be king in my marriage to Susan. She usually crowned me with a frying pan. In our marriage now, when I stepped up to become the priest and prophet of our family, she wanted to crown me king.

## The Father as Priest

The father as priest is revealed in Revelation 1:6: "Jesus Christ . . . has made us kings and priests to His God and Father, to Him be glory and dominion forever and ever." We have been formed into a kingdom, a royal race, as priests to our God. As the priest, the father or husband represents the family to God, and he is in the position—as spiritual head of the family—to ask God to bless the family. How does the father act as priest?

- He hears from God
- He represents his family's needs to God
- He blesses his family and talks to God about them, as in Job 1:5 where Job rises early in the morning to offer sacrifices for his family
- He prays about their spiritual experiences

How often do you hear someone say they were brought to Christ by the prayers of their father? Probably not often. You usually hear about the mother's prayers. Thank God for our mother's prayers. When I received Christ, my mother must have lost half of her prayer life. But what a blessing it could be for the body of Christ if we started hearing, "I changed my ways because of the prayers of my father." Dad has the authority as priest of his family because he represents his family to God and asks God to bless them. Susan and I pray daily that the children of the righteous shall turn to God. As I have taken my place as priest, I have the authority to go to God for my family.

Noah's family was rescued because of his righteousness. Compare Abraham with Lot in the Old Testament book of Genesis. There were two fathers. Lot blew it, but Abraham did great (think of the Abrahamic covenant we discussed in the second chapter). Abraham became the father of a mighty nation because he obeyed God and commanded his family to follow God. Lot, however, led his family into Sodom and Gomorrah, and he never got them out because of his disobedience. I wonder where we are leading our families today.

I spoke earlier about family-of-origin issues—that the sins of the father are passed down to the third and fourth generation. Joshua said, "Choose for yourselves this day whom you will serve . . . . But as for me and my house, we will serve the LORD" (Josh. 24:15 NKJV). Joshua's children were already grown when he said this. Instead of calling a family conference, he made a quality decision that his family was going to follow the Lord. God honored that kind of confession and determination, and Joshua's children respected him as leader of his family because he performed his priestly and prophetic ministry in the home. God will honor your leadership in the home as well.

## THE FATHER AS PROPHET

What does it mean that the father as prophet? It is not that the father gets a tremendous new revelation from God and passes it on to his family. God can do that, of course, but that is not the idea. Instead, the father as prophet presents God to his family by bringing the Word of God to them. The Lord wants fathers to reveal his nature to the family. That nature is flexible, loving, merciful, kind, tender, caring, and responsive. And God wants us as fathers to represent that godly nature. The prophet is one of the five fold ministries as in Ephesians 4:11.

Often a child's concept of God is formed by their earthly fathers. Working with couples in my practice, I find that many men have issues with competence because they might have heard shame or critical messages in childhood from their caretakers. That might have left those individuals feeling "less than" or "not good enough." This doesn't mean, however, that they are not competent. They could be extremely successful in their careers and still have a competency issue. I was successful in my career in show business and the business world, but inside I felt insecure and inadequate. I have worked with NFL and NBA athletes who rose to the top of their profession, and I know they often had insecurities. These issues often come from the relationship they had with their fathers.

Three aspects of a father as prophet are first, that he hears from God, second, he brings the Word of God to his family and represents his family to God, and third, he is responsible to teach or disciple his children to grow into responsible adults who have a relationship with God.

## The Father as King

Jesus is equal to the Father, but he submitted to the Father's headship. In the Old Testament, Eli was disqualified as high priest for Israel because his family did not submit to his headship. He did not command his house. It is important that husbands are the spiritual heads of their houses, leading their family in prayer, devotions, and modeling a relationship with Christ. The father needs to govern his family on behalf of God. The book of Genesis, speaking of Abraham, says, "For I have known (chosen, acknowledged) him [as My own], so that he may teach and command his children and the sons of his house after him to keep the way of the Lord and to do what is just and righteous, so that the Lord may bring Abraham what He has promised him" (18:19 AMPLIFIED). As husbands and fathers take their rightful role as godly men, teaching their families to keep the way of the Lord, they will truly be rewarded with the blessings of God.

God said he "sought a man among them who should build up the wall and stand in the gap before Me for the land, that I should not destroy it, but I found none" (Ezek. 22:30 AMPLIFIED). But the apostle Paul says in Philippians, "I have strength for all things in Christ, Who empowers me (4:13 AMPLIFIED). As fathers we have all the gifts to accomplish everything God has called us to do. But we have to say, "I will."

# Six Steps of Fulfilling God's Given Ministry of Priest, Prophet, and King

### 1. Recognize our position as father

Men need to face the fact that it is their responsibility to be the priest, prophet, and king of their families. There is no one else to fill that role. Fathers must accept that responsibility.

2. ADMIT OUR FAILURES

We need to admit it when we fail. That kind of transparency will cause our families to see us differently, with a godly humility. God can forgive our sins, but he cannot do anything about our excuses. For example, admit to your children that you were wrong when you did not make time for them. It takes a big man to admit his failures.

God has called us to be students. We take more training to drive a car than to get married and raise our children. Reading and studying the Word, and taking off our masks, will bring blessings to all in our families.

3. ACCEPT THE RESPONSIBILITY OF A PRIEST, PROPHET, AND KING

When we make that commitment, we need to realize that this journey requires us to get alone with God to hear from him.

4. REVIEW OUR PRIORITIES

If I see anything in our society today, it is misplaced priorities. That includes our church activities. So many churches have their parishioners involved in so many activities that couples hardly have any time for their own relationship. Often couples spend most of their time trying to be good parents, involving their kids in year-round activities or sports, so much so that they have no time for each other. The greatest gift we can give our children is first of all to model ourselves as a great husband or wife, and then second to be great parents.

Psalm 90:12 states, "So teach us to number our days, that we may get us a heart of wisdom" (AMPLIFIED). I suggest that readers list their responsibilities, which include one's relationship to spouse and family, job duties, the family activities, and any other responsibilities you have. Get these relationships firmly planted in the mind—and then test everything against biblical priorities. We might have to consider changing the image we have developed of ourselves, like Mr. Country Club, Mr. Fisherman, or Mr. Bank President.

## 5. Trust God for His Grace

Finding ways to activate faith is a must to achieve the ministry of priest, prophet, and king in our families. God will never take you where his grace is not with you.

## 6. God will honor the office of fatherhood when we step into that responsibility

If we have not previously taken on the office of fatherhood, be patient—as we develop new patterns of behavior, our family will notice that change and honor you for that. The sixth chapter of Ephesians tells us that children should "honor your father and mother, which is the first commandment with promise" (6:2 NKJV). This is the only commandment in the Bible linked to having a long life. What a gift to create the environment where our children can learn to honor their father and mother. That same Scripture in verse four tells us, "And you, fathers, do not provoke your children to wrath, but bring them up in the training and admonition of the Lord" (NKJV).

# The Proverbs 31 Wife

The first basic ingredient for a godly marriage and family is fatherhood. The next key is for the wife to become a virtuous woman, as described in Proverbs 31:

> Who can find a virtuous wife? For her worth is far above rubies. The heart of her husband safely trusts her; so he will have no lack of gain. She does him good and not evil all the days of her life. She seeks wool and flax, and willingly works with her hands. She is like the merchant ships, she brings her food from afar. She also rises while it is yet night, and provides food for her household, and a portion for her maidservants. She considers a field and buys it; from her profits she plants a vineyard. She girds herself with strength, and strengthens her arms. She perceives that her merchandise is good, and her lamp does not go out by night. She stretches out her hands to the distaff, and her hand holds the spindle. She extends her hand to the poor, yes, she reaches out her hands to the needy. She is not afraid of snow

for her household, for all her household is clothed with scarlet. She makes tapestry for herself; her clothing is fine linen and purple. Her husband is known in the gates, when he sits among the elders of the land. She makes linen garments and sells them, and supplies sashes for the merchants. Strength and honor are her clothing; she shall rejoice in time to come. She opens her mouth with wisdom, and on her tongue is the law of kindness. She watches over the ways of her household, and does not eat the bread of idleness. Her children rise up and call her blessed; her husband also, and he praises her: Many daughters have done well, but you excel them all." Charm is deceitful and beauty is passing, but a woman who fears the LORD, she shall be praised. Give her of the fruit of her hands, and let her own works praise her in the gates (31:10-31 NKJV).

Here are the characteristics that Scripture presents as goals for a godly wife. They are goals, and as such they are difficult to reach. But they can be reached, even in a painful marriage, one baby step at a time.

1. She is trustworthy. Trust is essential in a marriage. Proverbs 31:11 states, "The heart of her husband safely trusts her; so he will have no lack of gain" (NKJV). It is difficult for a man to achieve what he was meant to achieve, unless his wife trusts him. He will try to prove himself in his job, activities, or ministry, but what he really seeks is his wife's approval.
2. She is successful. A successful man mirrors his wife's success. He is a reflection of her accomplishments. Proverbs 31:23 states, "Her husband is known in the gates, when he sits among the elders of the land" (NKJV).
3. She is praiseworthy. A Proverbs 31 wife will have a husband who praises her. Verse 28 states, "Her children rise up and call her blessed; her husband also, and he praises her." A wife should be praiseworthy, as it is every man's duty to praise his wife for what she does for him. If the husband remains silent when the wife is praiseworthy, the Couples Dialogue mentioned in the fifth chapter would be a good thing to try.

4. She is to be extolled. A godly wife is the man's glory. You will know what kind of a man someone is when you meet his wife. The more content, restful, and healthy she is, the more stable the husband—as he can create the environment for that to happen. The moon has no glory without the sun shining on it. If the husband shines on his wife, she glows. If the husband is not shining on his wife, she will reflect that as well.

I think going to good marriage seminars can be very helpful—whether you have a good relationship or not. They can be excellent preparation for a vintage love relationship between the godly husband and the virtuous wife. They teach many helpful skills. When I have been seeing a couple in my practice, I use a relapse-prevention step before we terminate the therapy. I encourage them to continue the journey and use the skills I taught them in Imago Relationship Therapy. I advise them that they cannot put the information away in the bottom of a drawer and expect the change to become permanent.

The way a husband can love his wife in the way Christ loves the church is to become the priest, prophet, and spiritual head of his household. This can be done by honoring, valuing, respecting, trusting, and listening to his wife. Wives must begin this journey as well by honoring, valuing, respecting, trusting, and listening to their husbands. Learn to use the couple's dialogue of mirroring, validating, and showing empathy.

Husbands, rediscover the attitude of courtship. I am going to court my wife for the rest of our days on this earth. Move from being relationally lazy or complacent to focusing on the relationship and making it your priority. Learn more about the godly idea of marriage covenant. Make the space between you safe and sacred instead of toxic. Have devotions and pray together.

Perhaps then, we will be the model for our children that God intends, and we will see them grow up to have healthy marriages and children of their own. We are already praying for our grandchildren's spouses. You can have the relationship of your dreams. We have it every day, and when we have a disagreement, we repair it and forgive each other. You already have permission to do it.

## Chapter Ten

# HOW TO TURN THE FIZZLE BACK INTO A SIZZLE!

### Humor and Happiness

THE COUPLES I see in my counseling practice often have so much pain, and it is sometimes difficult for them to see that they can have real love and laughter. Some grow up in a spontaneous environment with their families while others might have grown up in a serious environment. But when we have laughter and humor in our relationships, it allows us to break up the previously frozen (rigid) perceptions of our partner, ourselves, and our relationships. Including humor and happiness in our lives and relationships will create an endorphin bath. Endorphins have peptides, which give us a feeling of well-being and security. I call them God's anti-depressant.

John Bradshaw stated that "Humor is a shift of perception that gives people the guts to go on when life looks its worst . . . There is an abandonment in it that is close to enlightenment. It lifts suffering off the heart and hands it to the intellect and spirit, which alone has the power to heal it." Humor can invigorate our lives.

### Why Have Fun?

The ancient Greek philosopher Aristotle, in *The Nicomachean Ethics,* stated that "happiness is the whole aim and end of human existence."

When we have fun and laugh, we experience our life more fully. Earlier I wrote of John Bradshaw stating, "We were never intended to lose our childhood traits; we were intended to maximize them in adult life." Those traits include being playful, carefree, and fun loving. When we laugh, we drop our defenses and are open to experiencing our connection to each other and the world we live in. Humor shifts our perspective. *Psychology Today*, a mental wellness magazine, had an article called "Laughter is the Best Medicine." According to the article, laughter has these benefits:

1. It reduces pain and allows us to tolerate discomfort.
2. It reduces blood sugar levels, increasing glucose tolerance in diabetics and nondiabetics alike.
3. It improves job performance, especially if our work depends on creativity and solving complex problems. Although its role in intimate relationships is vastly underestimated, it really is the glue of good marriage. It synchronizes the brains of a speaker and listener so they are emotionally attuned.
4. Laughter establishes—or restores—a positive emotional climate and a sense of connection between two people. In fact some researchers believe that the major function of laughter is to bring people together. All the health benefits of laughter may simply result from the social support that laughter stimulates.
5. Laughter may even help our blood vessels function better. New evidence shows laughter acts on the inner lining of blood vessels, called the endothelium, causing the vessels to relax and expand, increasing blood flow. In other words, laughter is good for the heart and brain, two organs that require the blood's steady flow of oxygen.

When I meet with counselees, I engage the whole person: spirit, soul, and body. The soul is the mind, emotions, and will. When we take care of the whole person, we can reach the potential that God has for us. To help guide you toward the whole person—which includes fun and humor in life—I invite you to write the answers to the following sentence stems:

In my family growing up,

Fun was . . .

Joy was . . .

Laughter was . . .

My thoughts around these memories right now while I am writing this are . . .

You can use these sentence stems with your partner to share noncontroversial information to create connection and intimacy. Some other "happiness activities" include expressing gratitude to each other, practicing acts of kindness, learning to forgive, savoring life's goals, spending time with God and the Bible, committing to achieving certain goals, and taking care of our bodies.

## Intentional Steps

If we make intentional steps toward creating this type of relationship, you can have the relationship of your dreams! In other words, we only get a return out of what we put in. The way to create the relationship of your dreams is to build new habits with the ways we relate to each other. Consider this:

### Habit

I am your constant companion.
I am your greatest asset or heaviest burden.
I will push you up to success or down to disappointment.
I am at your command.
Half the things you do might just as well be turned over to me,
for I can do them quickly, correctly, and profitably.
I am easily managed, just be firm with me.
Those who are great, I have made great.

Those who are failures, I have made failures.
I am not a machine, though I work with the precision of a machine and the intelligence of a person.
You can run me for profit, or you can run me for ruin.
Show me how you want it done. Educate me. Train me.
Lead me. Reward me.
And I will then . . . do it automatically.
I am your servant.
Who am I?
I am a habit.
(Author Unknown)

## 61 Starter Ideas to Increase Romance and Passion

Using ideas like these can help you turn the fizzle back into a sizzle and overcome the tendency to become relationally complacent. One day after reading the following list of starter ideas to increase romance, I came home and sat in front of my wife. I lifted her feet in my lap, and began rubbing her feet. This is not one of my favorite things. At first she asked if I had lost my mind. I said, "No. I am going to have an affair with you." She just sat back and enjoyed the journey.

Do you feel like you have fallen out of love with your spouse or life partner? Dawn J. Lipthrott, a fellow Imago Relationship Therapist and friend in Winter Park, Florida, has put together this wonderful list of ideas. Dawn has so many creative ideas, and she gave me permission to use this.

1. Call your partner unexpectedly just to say you love them and were thinking of them.
2. Call your spouse/partner just to tell them one thing you appreciate about them.
3. Send your spouse/partner flowers at home, at the office, or away at a hotel room "just because," or to say "thank-you," or "because I love you."
4. Send a fax or email to work saying you love your partner and can't wait to be with him/her again.
5. Pick up flowers or dinner on the way home and surprise your partner.

6. Call your partner at 10:00 AM and say you want to take him/her out to lunch.
7. When you come home, find your partner and just hold him/her close for a moment for a prolonged hug—no words necessary.
8. When you walk by your partner at home, touch him/her or give a hug or a caress.
9. Wake up to the day as if it was the first time you were alone with your spouse. Greet him/her enthusiastically. Sit and just look lovingly at him/her for a few moments. Ask about them and their plans for the day and just listen and try to let them know you understand (even if you disagree)—no problem-solving unless asked for.
10. Write a note and put it where your partner will find it during the day. Tell him/her loving things.
11. List ten things you love about your partner or your relationship and leave it where they will find it (or mail it to him/her).
12. Try a new way to make your lovemaking more sensual and prolonged. (Try using candles, incense, longer foreplay, times of just kissing and holding, caressing, and exploring each other's bodies by touch.)
13. Make love with no penetration—be creative in being sexually loving.
14. When you go to bed, sleep nude together, without sex. Just hold your spouse or snuggle next to him/her so your bodies touch. (Also good with pajamas/nightgown on.)
15. Bring home balloons (or hide them and put them out at night after your partner goes to bed) with a note or sign with something like "I celebrate you," "You are wonderful," or something similar.
16. Pamper your partner one evening. (For example: if watching TV, ask your partner if he/she would like anything—offer to put a stool under their feet or take off their shoes and massage their feet. If cooking dinner, volunteer to clean up and do dishes while your partner just relaxes. Give a back rub. Put on soothing music, or other things.)
17. Next time you kiss, pause, and look into your partner's eyes, remembering what it was like when you first met. Touch his/

her face. Trace his/her lips with your finger. Slowly bring your lips to theirs—first gently kissing his/her upper lip, then lower lip. Embrace your partner and gently kiss them fully, letting your lips part, and enjoy every second of it. After the kissing is finished, just hold each other a few moments longer.
18. Plan a date. Arrange for a baby-sitter and clear your calendar. (It's good to do this one once a week or at least every two weeks.)
19. "Surprise" your partner by taking them someplace they have said they wanted to go—a sporting event, a concert, a restaurant, a computer show, the mall, or someplace else. Do it even if it isn't something you like. Enjoy your partner enjoying it and simply do it for love.
20. List ten romantic things to say to your partner, and say them from time to time throughout the week.
21. Create a romantic dinner—either out or in.
22. Take a bath together with bath oils or bubbles and candles.
23. Do what you would do for an anniversary on a regular day—just because.
24. Buy a gift for your partner—it can be a blouse or shirt he/she wanted or something simple and inexpensive.
25. Plan a picnic in the park (or your own yard or living room)
26. Even when you still have chores to do, take the day off and go to a movie or do something else fun.
27. Call your partner unexpectedly during the day (or at night if they are out of town) and talk sexy to him/her, telling them how much you long to feel him/her.
28. Plan a surprise getaway weekend for just the two of you—arranging for baby-sitters or dog-sitters. Take your partner someplace you think he or she will love. You can go to a nice hotel in your own city!
29. Greet your partner at the airport with a balloon or flower and an enthusiastic "welcome home."
30. Take out an ad in the Lost and Found with something like "I've found love with you," or something similar. Have a florist deliver a rose, the newspaper, and a note telling him/her which page to turn to and where the ad is.

31. Arrange things so your partner can sleep in one weekend morning. Take care of the telephone, kids, dogs, and other distractions.
32. Leave your favorite romantic song (perhaps from when you first dated) on your partner's voice mail or answering machine.
33. Give your spouse a message on any part or all of his/her body (if full body, create the right climate with candles and such).
34. Sit and talk about fun and romantic times in your relationship—when you were dating, first married, and other times. Enjoy the memories and think about how to bring some of that into the present.
35. Write a short poem (even if it doesn't rhyme and even if you think you could never write poetry) telling of your love. You can start with lines like, "Like the light of a harvest moon...," "Heart to heart...," "Like the water caresses the sand...," or other romantic sentiments.
36. Lip sync a romantic song for your partner after dinner one night.
37. Bring home or to the office your partner's favorite sweet thing.
38. Leave a flower on the pillow before your partner goes to bed—even if it is one you pick from your own yard.
39. Plan a "secret rendezvous" in your own town, or in the city where your partner is on business.
40. Take the afternoon off and just go someplace together.
41. Send your partner a postcard when you are out of town saying you were thinking of him/her and love him/her. It doesn't matter if you get home before the postcard does.
42. Write a love letter as if you were just falling in love with the person.
43. Tell your partner that instead of watching TV tonight (or doing work, or fussing with the kids), you simply want to be with them.
44. Go for a walk together after dinner, holding hands and remembering good times you've had.
45. Write "I love you" on the bathroom mirror with lipstick or shaving cream.
46. Shower together.
47. Paint a heart or something else on your partner's body with whipped cream or chocolate syrup, and lick it off slowly, and say Mmmm.

48. Tell your partner before you go to bed, or before you leave in the morning, one of the things you love about him/her (a quality, a physical characteristic, a behavior).
49. Agree to meet at a social event or public place and act as if you are meeting each other for the first time—flirt, "make eyes" at each other, gesture from across the room, or rub against each other when walking by.
50. Go skinny dipping in your pool or hot tub.
51. Test drive a Porsche or a convertible with the top down and pretend you are seeing each other although it has been forbidden by your parents. Drive safely! If you want to kiss, pull over!
52. When your partner is coming home late in the evening, have your bed turned down, a hot bath ready with flower petals floating in it, and candles lit.
53. Rent a video you know your spouse would like or has liked in the past, make popcorn, and have an evening together like teenagers.
54. Create your own "slumber party" for just the two of you.
55. Drive to the beach (or spend the night there) and go for walks on the beach holding hands.
56. When you have to go out of town on business, add an extra day and invite your spouse to join you for all or part of your trip.
57. Undress your spouse as if it were the first time—slowly, touching their body as you go.
58. Make sexy, loving comments to your spouse throughout the evening.
59. After dinner, or after the kids go to bed, put on one of your or your partner's favorite slow songs—or the song from your wedding—take her or him by the hand, and slow dance, relishing the feeling of it and the memories with it.
60. Text your spouse and tell them how "hot" they are.
61. Use your imagination—this is a person you are just falling in love with (again)—be creative in ways to express that.

Take these ideas, surprise your partner, and enjoy the relationship of your dreams.

# BIBLIOGRAPHY

Fisher, Helen. *The Anatomy of Love* (New York: Ballantine, 1992).

Gottman, John M. *The Seven Principles for Making Marriage Work* (New York: Crown, 1999).

Gray, John. *Men Are From Mars, Women Are From Venus* (New York: HarperCollins, 1992).

Hendrix, Harville. *Getting the Love You Want.* (New York: Harper Perennial, 1988).

Hendrix, Harville. *Keeping the Love You Find* (New York: Pocket Books, 1992).

Hendrix, Harville. *Getting the Love You Want: A Guide for Couples* (New York: St. Martin's, 2007).

Liebowitz, Michael, M.D. *The Chemistry of Love* (Boston: Little, Brown, 1983).

Love, Pat. *The Truth About Love* (New York: Fireside, 2001).

Love, Pat. *How To Improve Your Marriage Without Talking About It* (New York: Broadway Books, 2007).

McGee, Robert, Pat Springle, Jim Craddock, and Dale W. McCleskey, *Breaking the Cycle of Hurtful Family Experiences* (Nashville: Rapha, 1994).

Mahler, Margaret. *On Human Symbiosis and the Vicissitudes of Individuation: Infantile Psychosis* (New York: Intern Universities, 1968).

Donald Nathanson. *Shame and Pride* (New York: W.W. Norton & Co., March 17, 1994).

*Psychology Today* bi-monthly magazine.

Rath, Tom and James K. Harter. *Wellbeing* (Washington, D.C.: Gallup, 2009).

Roberts, Richard Owen, *Repentance* (Wheaton: Crossway Books 2002)

Simon, Sidney and Suzanne Simon, *Forgiveness, How to Make Peace with Your Past* (New York: Grand Central, 1991).

Sledge, Tim. *Moving Beyond Your Past* (Nashville: Life Way, 1994).

Garland, Diana, S. Richmond, and Betty Hassler, Southern Baptist Convention. *Covenant Marriage* (Nashville: Life Way, 1992).

Spring, Janis Abrahms. *After the Affair* (New York: HarperCollins, 1996).

Vaughan, Peggy. *The Monogamy Myth.* (New York: Newmarket Press 1989)

# ENDNOTES

**Chapter One**

1. Matthew George Easton, *Easton's Bible Dictionary*. (Web site: www.forgottenbooks.org, 2007). Three Greek words are used in the New Testament to denote repentance. The first is the verb *metamelomai*, which is used of a change of mind (such as to feel remorse on account of sin) but not necessarily a change of heart. This word is used with reference to the repentance of Judas: "When Judas, who had betrayed him, saw that Jesus was condemned, he was seized with remorse and returned the thirty silver coins to the chief priests and the elders. (Matt. 27:3 NIV). The second verb is *metanoeo,* meaning to change one's mind and purpose. Third is the cognate noun *metanoia,* which is used of true repentance, a change of mind and purpose and life, to which remission of sin is promised.

**Chapter Two**

1. Garland, Diana, S. Richmond, and Betty Hassler, Southern Baptist Convention, *Covenant Marriage* (Nashville: Life Way, 1992). P. 14-15 (Reprinted and used by permission)
2. Ibid., P.22-23

3. Ibid., P.26-30
4. Ibid., P.30-32

**Chapter Three**

1. Helen Fisher, *The Anatomy of Love* (New York: Ballantine Publishing Group, 1992).
2. Harville Hendrix, *Getting the Love You Want* (New York: Harper Perennial, 1988).P. 47-64
3. Pat Love, *The Truth About Love* (New York: Fireside, 2001). P. 28-29
4. Michael Liebowitz, *The Chemistry of Love* (Boston: Little, Brown, 1983).
5. *Ibid.*
6. John Gottman, *The Seven Principles for Making Marriage Work* (New York: Crown Publishers, 1999). P. 27-34

**Chapter Four**

1. Harville Hendrix, *Getting the Love You Want* (New York: Harper Perennial, 1988).
2. *Ibid.*
3. *Ibid*
4. Paul McLean, Man and His Animal Brain, Modern Medicine 32, 1964 P. 95-106
5. Harville Hendrix, *Getting the Love You Want* (New York: Harper Perennial, 1988)

**Chapter Five**

1. John Bradshaw, *Healing the Shame that Binds You* (Deerfield Beach, Fla.: HCI, 1988). P. 5 and 43
2. Pat Love, *How To Improve Your Marriage Without Talking About It* (New York: Broadway Books, 2007). P. 10-20

**Chapter Six**

1. Roberts, Richard Owen. *Repentance* (Wheaton:Crossway Books 2002) P. 105-132

2. Sidney and Suzanne Simon, *Forgiveness, How to Make Peace with Your Past* (New York: Grand Central Publishing, 1991) P. 9-21

## Chapter Seven

1. Vaughan, Peggy, *The Monogamy Myth.* (New York: Newmarket Press 1989)
2. Sonny Shulkin, David and Donna Bowman: I have merged their ideas with some of my own and have permission to use the ideas.

## Chapter Nine

1. Spring, Janet Abram, *After the Affair.* (New York: Harper Collins 1997) P. 75

To order additional copies of this book call:
1-877-421-READ (7323)
or please visit our website at
www.WinePressbooks.com

If you enjoyed this quality custom-published book,
drop by our website for more books and information.

www.winepresspublishing.com
"Your partner in custom publishing."

CPSIA information can be obtained at www.ICGtesting.com
Printed in the USA
LVOW121801041012

301527LV00006B/216/P